UNDERSTANDING BIBLE TEACHING

God's World

Arthur E Cundall BA, BD

Scripture Union

47 Marylebone Lane, London W1 6AX

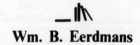

Wm. B. Eerdmans

225 Jefferson Avenue, Grand Rapids, Michigan

© 1971 Scripture Union
First published 1971
Reprinted 1973
First published in this form 1978

ISBN 0 85421 717 7 (Scripture Union)
ISBN 0 8028 1759 9 (Wm. B. Eerdmans)

Printed in Great Britain at the Benham Press
by William Clowes & Sons Limited, Colchester and Beccles

General Introduction

There are many commentaries on the Biblical text and there are many systematic studies of Christian doctrine, but these studies are unique in that they comment on selected passages relating to the major teachings of the Bible. The comments are designed to bring out the doctrinal implications rather than to be a detailed verse by verse exposition, but writers have always attempted to work on the basis of sound exegetical principles. They have also aimed to write with a certain devotional warmth, and to demonstrate the contemporary relevance of the teaching.

These studies were originally designed as a daily Bible reading aid and formed part of Scripture Union's Bible Characters and Doctrines series. They can, of course, still be used in this way but experience has shown that they have a much wider use. They have a continued usefulness as a summary and exposition of Biblical teaching arranged thematically, and will serve as a guide to the major passages relating to a particular doctrine.

Writers have normally based their notes on the RSV text but readers will probably find that most modern versions are equally suitable. Many, too, have found them to be an excellent basis for group Bible study. Here the questions and themes for further study and discussion will prove particularly useful—although many individuals will also find them stimulating and refreshing.

ONE

The Beginnings

1 : Faith the Key

Hebrews 11.1–6

It is appropriate that we should begin this series of studies on 'God in His World' by considering the place of faith. Faith, to the writer to the Hebrews, is that spirit of utmost confidence in God which touches life at its every point. In **10**.38, quoting Hab. **2**.4, he recalls God's words, 'my righteous one shall live by faith'; now he proceeds to define faith. His definition is not, of course, an alternative to that of the Pauline epistles, where faith is personal trust in Christ as Saviour (it is usually accepted that Paul was not the author of Hebrews). Paul would most certainly agree that 'faith apart from works is dead' (Jas. **2**.26, cf. Eph. **2**.10). The witness of the whole Bible is that faith is a relationship with God which influences every aspect of life. Faith is essential in our *worship*, as in the case of Abel (4). It is unnecessary to ask whether this verse means that Abel, because of his faith, offered a richer sacrifice to God, or that his sacrifice was the more acceptable to God because of his faith. Careful thought will show the truth of each alternative, but in context the second is preferable. Faith is essential in our daily *walk*, as in the case of Enoch, who walked with God and so pleased Him (5, cf. Gen. **5**.22 ff.). It is essential too in the maintenance of a consistent *witness*, especially when it

5

involves proclaiming judgement in a difficult age, as in the case of Noah (7).

The two main spheres of faith, the future and the unseen, are noted in v. 1. Faith has unbounded assurance in the ultimate fulfilment of God's will and promises (cf. **11**.11). In this realm it loses all sense of uncertainty, because it is based on the assurance that what God has promised He is able to perform. Faith has also an unclouded conviction of the present reality of the unseen God and the spiritual forces He employs (cf. 2 Cor. **4**.18). But it also affects our view of our present world, with all its awe-inspiring grandeur and complexity, as called into being by the creative act of God (3). Man, in his quest for understanding, has thought hard and long about this, but the Bible, whilst asserting the fact of a Creator-God, does not satisfy our natural curiosity concerning the mechanics of creation. This bears on our future studies, for when we have read everything written about creation we must still make the reverent admission of v. 3. The need for a faith of this kind comes as a challenge in a sceptical age.

The centrality of faith in God, the great unseen Reality confronting us, is further underlined (6). 'Draw near' is a semi-technical term indicating the drawing near to God in worship (e.g. Heb. **10**.21 f.). The reward of the divine blessing still comes to those who 'draw near', who believe passionately in God, that this world is His world, and who seek to know more of God Himself and His relationship to the world.

2 : 'In the beginning'
Genesis 1.1–2.3

The first eleven chapters of Genesis are a miracle of compression. When we reach **12**.1 we experience a sense of leisureliness as the story of God's redemptive activity begins with His call to Abraham, to whom more than thirteen chapters are devoted. Yet in the eleven opening chapters we discover all that is necessary for understanding what follows: the relation of God to His world and to man; the relation of man to the world and his fellow men; the fact of sin and its effect upon the God-man and man-man relationships; the inevitability of divine judgement on man's wilful and continued sin and the ever-present fact of the divine grace. In this sense these chapters have been described as a prologue to the entire Bible. This estimate accepts the historicity of the events recorded, but indicates also the importance of the great spiritual and theological truths they teach.

The creation narrative stands in a solitary grandeur when compared with its heathen counterparts, with their unsavoury details of the amours and intrigues of the gods. No attempt to explain God is made. He is introduced as the uncreated, eternally-existent, transcendent One (1). Dualism of any kind is excluded, for God is not set over against already-existent matter, He creates the world 'out of nothing' (*ex nihilo*) and all creation is related to Him and to no other power (cf. John 1.3). Thus, at the very beginning, God stands uniquely apart and yet intimately related to each part of His creation.

Note the distinction between the references to productivity in the plant world (12) and reproduction in birds and fishes (22) and man (28), the latter resulting from a special divine act of blessing. Sexual reproduction is here given a sacred function as a special gift or endowment. Man especially, in keeping with the remainder of the Biblical revelation (cf. Psa. **8**), is given a worthy place (26). 'Let us make man' may be no more than the 'royal we', but it may hint at the heavenly host (cf. **3**.22; **11**.7; 1 Kings **22**.19; Isa. **6**.8) which was informed of so significant an act. 'In our image' includes much more than physical characteristics, for, to the Hebrew, the body was part of, and expressive of, the total being. The phrase involves spiritual powers and the capacity for communion. From these lofty heights man fell catastrophically, due to his sin (cf. Heb. **2**.6–9), but the same condescending love and grace which created man opened up a way of salvation and restoration to the original creative purpose. Two further points may be briefly mentioned: 1. the prominence given to the Sabbath (**2**.2 f.) underlines its universal, permanent significance; 2. the fact that God 'saw that it was good' (**1**.10, 12, 18, 21, 25, 31) allows a certain optimism which even the blemishes caused by 'man's inhumanity to man' cannot eradicate.

3 : God and Man

Genesis 2.4–24

Apart from Isaiah, Jeremiah, Job and the Psalmist the allusions in the O.T. to God as the Creator are rare. The reason is that to Israel He was revealed chiefly as the God of Salvation, and it is His saving-acts in history which dominated Hebrew thought. Nevertheless, the *fact* of God as Creator, especially of man, is assumed throughout the O.T., and forms the foundation of its doctrine of man, and of the God-man relationship.

Gen. 2.4–24 is not, as it has been commonly supposed, an alternative or contradictory account of creation. Many of the essential elements in creation, carefully noted in ch. 1, are missing. Instead of its precise cosmic statement, we find here a concentration upon man and his environment. Clearly, it is to be connected with the account of the fall of man in ch. 3 (cf. the use of the divine name 'Lord God' throughout). The setting of man, his relationship to his wife and the detail concerning the tree of life (16 f.) are all indispensable to an understanding of ch. 3. Nevertheless, the particular care which God here shows to man underlines the fact noted in ch. 1, that man is the climax of creation, and the intimacy of the God-man relationship illustrates the assertion that 'God created man in his own image' (1.27). In both chapters God is manifestly the sole Creator, and especially the Giver of Life. He gives the breath of life (7) to man and he lives (cf. Ezek. 37.7–10). He withdraws His Spirit, and man dies (cf. Psa. 104.29 f; Eccl. 12.7). Man, therefore, is distinct from his Creator; he is formed from common materials (7) in contrast to the transcendent, uncreated Deity. Man is a spirit-animated body, and both elements, spirit and body, are necessary to existence. This has an important bearing upon other O.T. doctrines, e.g. that of the resurrection. To the Hebrew, a bodily resurrection was essential.

The O.T., therefore, invests man with true personal dignity and a mission of responsibility as well as dependence. Separate from the animal creation (note how he names them, 19) and lower than God, he could be fearfully alone. But God, in His gracious love, gave him the woman to stand beside him as his counterpart. The relationship of the sexes in the divine will, with the womanly dependence matched by a complete sharing, is here noted (20-24). And man is given a test of his moral and spiritual responsibility (16 f.). God, we might have thought, took a terrible risk, but He knew what He was doing. Spontaneous, responsible communion was preferred to the mechanical response of the automatons He *could* have created.

Implications

4: Does God Care?

Job 10.8–22

Job's vision was clouded by the extreme suffering which he endured, and the badgering he received at the hands of his friends did little to relieve his sense of utter desolation. Yet we can detect what Job *felt* to be the truth about the relationship between God and himself, even though his predicament seemed to make a mockery of his beliefs.

God was his Creator (8–12). The process of conception and the growth of the embryo in the womb are seen as His creative work (cf. Psa. 139.13–16). But there is more in mind than the mere artistry of a designer; a loving care dominates all, both before and after birth (12). God, in Job's estimate, was, or *ought* to have been, a tender, gracious Heavenly Father, although the darkness of his experience made an apparent travesty of such a relationship. Moreover, there is an underlying belief that God is righteous, indicated by Job's indignant protest that, irrespective of whether he is righteous or unrighteous, God appears to have an inflexible purpose to destroy him (13–17). This *ought not* to be so, Job feels, if God is true to His character. A second implication of this section is that sin affects the relationship with God (cf. Gen. 3; Isa. 59.2). This Job readily allows, though convinced of his own integrity. So keenly does he feel the apparent incongruity of God's dealings with him, that he avows that he would have been better unborn or stillborn (18 f.). He was not to know at this stage that, through suffering, he was demonstrating (*a*) to the accuser, that man was capable of an unbought loyalty to God (cf. 1.9 ff.); (*b*) to that strength of personal relationship

9

existing between a godly man and his Maker. *Never* could Job accept that God did not exist.

Job, along with others in the O.T. period, did not grasp at this time that this relationship with God extended beyond the grave (21 f., cf. Isa. **38**.18 f.). But there were O.T. saints who knew that God's sovereign power included Sheol, the realm beyond death (cf. Psa. **139**.8; Amos **9**.2) and that even death could not destroy the relationship of fellowship which the godly man enjoyed with Him (Psa. **16**.10 f., **49**.15; **73**.24 ff.). Job himself, through the very pressure of his circumstances, was ultimately to come to experience the same precious truth (cf. the two stages of **14**.13–17; **19**.23–27 and note also **26**.6).

5 : How Little We Know !

Job 26

In the previous chapter Bildad had developed the theme of the omnipotence and transcendence of God, in contrast with puny man. His view is not without its dangers. Granted that man is finite, and insignificant in comparison with his Creator, this does not mean that he is automatically unclean and thereby excluded from God, nor incapable of any moral or spiritual relationship with Him. But Job takes up Bildad's general line of argument, which he can set forth just as adequately. It is not this kind of lecture he needs, but rather sympathy, understanding and strength (2–4). These he does not find from his friends. He was, eventually, to find what he was seeking from God Himself (chs. **38–41**), and through ways which were very similar to the outlook propounded by Bildad, and here by Job himself.

Job freely admits his weakness (2 f.), which contrasts with the sovereign power of God, who has control of the netherworld and its occupants (5 f.), even over Abaddon, the lowest region of Sheol (cf. Prov. **15**.11). He is also Lord of heaven and earth (7-11). This magnificent description uses the figurative language of the ancient world; the earth floating on the great deep, so that the underworld was under the waters (cf. v. 5); the inverted dome of the sky, its rim resting on the great mountains ('the pillars of heaven,' 11) and dividing between the regions of light and darkness (10); the clouds, like giant water-skins (8, cf. **38**.4–7). But the great point of this description is theological. Everything is dependent upon God and subject to His will. Notice the many verbs denoting His activity. In vs. 12 f. Job goes beyond the mere description of the natural world and employs the language of the ancient creation-myths, particularly concerning the mythical dragon, Rahab or Leviathan, the personification of the sea and the powers of chaos (cf. **3**.8; Isa. **27**.1; **51**.9, etc.). This reference, in company with the other biblical writers, he uses in a purely illustrative way, to indicate that the rule of God is absolute, there can be no challenge to His power.

The chapter concludes with an admission, in the form of a psalm celebrating the divine transcendence, that when we have exhausted the capacity of human thought and language to describe the wonders of God's creative and sustaining acts, we comprehend but the 'outskirts of his ways' (14). Moses was allowed to see but a fraction of that glory (Exod. **33**.18–23) and Isaiah glimpsed only its fringe (Isa. **6**.1). But both men were transformed by their experiences. Similarly, we must realize that our carefully formulated theological propositions fall far short of the full measure of God's glory and grace. Nature and theology, these are an incomplete reflection, not the full revelation, which came in the Person of Jesus Christ (cf. Matt. **11**.27; John **14**. 8 ff; Col. **1**.15–19).

6 : God and the Inanimate World

Job 38.1–38

Some scholars have expressed disappointment with the 'Yahweh speeches' in Job (chs. **38–41**). God, they feel, does not deal sympathetically with Job's acute distress, but rather batters him with questions. Such reasoning misses completely the sublime revelation of God and His ways in these chapters, which lifts the whole problem from the finite level of man to his Creator's infinite level. Job, burdened by affliction, had misrepresented God as unjust and indifferent (e.g. **9**.13–19; **19**.6–12). He was in danger of something less than humility, indeed he conceived himself as approaching God on virtually equal terms (cf. **31**.37). The Yahweh speeches show the immense gap between a man and his Creator but underline the grace of God which leads Him to communicate with man. By His immeasurable wisdom in the creation of both the inanimate world (**38**.4–38) and the animal creation (**38**.39–**39**.30), Job is to understand that his sufferings are not due to God's ignorance, and the evidence of meticulous care and forethought in His creation ought to convince Job that his adversity serves some purpose in God's beneficent will (cf. **23**.10).

Other truths also come to light in this sublime poem. The *eternal existence* of the Creator is everywhere implied; He was there at the very beginning (4). The *miracle* of creation is apparent—man does not understand the mysteries of the creation of the earth (4–7); the sea (8–11); night and day (12–15); the depths of Sheol or the immensity of the earth (16 ff.); light and darkness (19 ff.); the elements of the weather (22–30, 34–38) and the stars (31 ff.). But nature, which can appear so fearful a foe to the heathen, has no terror for the man who realizes that all is subject to God. The *essential goodness* of this God-made universe is clearly revealed (cf. Gen. 1.31). It is to be enjoyed by man—nowhere in Scripture is there any warrant for the view that matter is evil, and this world a prison-house of the soul. There is a hint, too, of a point we shall notice in our later studies, viz. the *Lordship of God in history* (22 f., cf. Josh. **10**.11; Psa. **18**.12 ff.; Isa. **30**.30; Ezek. **13**.11 ff.). The superabundant goodness of God, which takes in all creation, not simply that sector affecting man, is shown in vs. 25 ff. (cf. Matt. **5**.45). Man calls this Providence, but behind it there is a personal God. The inference of these chapters is that men, contemplating these aspects of creation, may learn something of God (cf. Rom. **1**.18–23).

7 : God and the Animal Creation

Job 38.39—39.30

Possibly Job and his friends were at fault in regarding this world as exclusively man-centred, with everything designed to subserve their own needs. With the exception of the horse (19–25) all the creatures mentioned are the least amenable or accessible to man, who does not provide their food nor understand fully their ways. The survey passes rapidly from one remote area to another : the lions (38.39 f.); the ravens of the desolate areas, whose food supply seems so precarious (38.41); the mountain goats, renowned for their 'wariness and wildness' (Tristram, 39.1–4); the wild ass, the very epitome of unrestrained freedom (39.5–8); the untameable wild ox (39.9–12); the ostrich, proverbial for its cruelty to its young (39.16, cf. Lam. 4.3) and its stupidity (39.17), so unlike man, especially in the apparent absence of any capacity to love (39.13 f.), and yet able to outpace man and so preserve itself (39.18); the war-horse, whose noble qualities man can utilize but not create (39.19–25); the hawk, with its migratory instincts (39.26) and, finally, the eagle, dwelling in inaccessible eyries and characterized by incredibly sharp vision and ferocity. All these creatures behave in ways alien to man, but God perfectly understands them, provides for them, and fits them individually for survival.

This respect for the animal creation is documented elsewhere in the O.T. The working ox is not to be muzzled (Deut. 25.4) and there are even laws governing bird-nesting (Deut. 22.6 f.). Isaiah describes the ox and ass as loyal servants of man (1.3) and envisages the day when the animal-creation will share in the Messianic kingdom (11.6–9). Israelite law legislated for kindness towards animals (Exod. 23.4 f.; Deut. 22.4) and against that gross abuse of animals prevalent amongst the Canaanites (Lev. 18.23, cf. 20.15 f.). Our own generation needs to discover the preciousness of all life. The indiscriminate slaughter of animals for man's pleasure in hunting, or for the luxury market in furs, and at least some of the intensive methods used to rear living creatures of all types for the food-table, show that some men regard them as existing solely for man's use. The Scriptures make it plain that while God allows man to use the animal creation for food, this has its limits. Man is of more value than a sparrow, but God still cares for the sparrow (Matt. 10.29 ff.).

8 : 'How Great Thou Art'

Job 40; 42.1–6

Some commentators have accused God of 'nagging' Job in the second Divine-Speech (40.6–41.34) following Job's apparent submission (40.3 ff.). It is important therefore to see what was involved in Job's 'submission', and why God pursued His questions. By this stage Job had become aware of his own littleness. His preoccupation with his own concerns, his protestations of his own righteousness and the injustice of God (cf. Job 9.22 ff.) have disappeared, and he sees his appropriate place in God's complex, orderly world. But there is no trace of positive repentance, nor sorrow at his slandering of the Almighty.

So God continues to question Job. In the first speech the emphasis is on the divine wisdom, in the second on the divine power, with the inference that Job's afflictions were not due to any divine inability. The main purpose is to bring Job into a right relationship with God on the basis of a right appreciation of Him. There is a gentle irony in 40.7–14. Will Job, who had so falsely represented God, and regarded himself as the virtual equal of God, *act* like God? If he can, then God will acknowledge Job's right to seek his own vindication and salvation (14). The passage is a powerful witness to the inadequacy of man to effect his own salvation by works. The remainder of the chapter gives a vigorous description of but one of God's creatures, Behemoth, probably the hippopotamus (cf. the description of Leviathan, usually identified with the crocodile, in ch. 41). Notice the gentle humour throughout, a sure indication that God was *not* brow-beating Job.

In the light of the total revelation Job was brought to a true repentance (42.1–6), realizing that God's question (38.2) fitted him perfectly. Like Isaiah in the Temple (Isa. 6.5) and Peter in the fishing boat (Luke 5.8), it was the revelation of God's majesty which made Job aware of his sin, not the sin of evil deeds, but the sin of misrepresenting God. Until now his knowledge of God had been partly academic and second-hand; now there was a new reality, and finiteness trembled in the presence of the Infinite. Job's self-centred world had expanded to take in God, and his apparently-unjust suffering was a problem no more. Most human problems become less acute in the light of His glory and grace! The book of Job witnesses to the loving wisdom and power of the Creator God, but also reveals the nature of the personal communion between God and Man. It is not a relationship of equality in which man can argue or assert his rights; it is one of grace. The basic O.T. definition of religion is 'the fear of God' (cf Psa. **19**.9; **34**.11; Prov. **1**.7; Jer. **32**.40), not a slavish, abject fear, but a reverential awe which takes into account God's majesty and holiness.

Questions and themes for study and discussion on Studies 1–8

1. Arising from the note on Heb. **11**.1–6, consider the implications of the word 'believer'.

2. Can the world as we know it still be described as 'good' (Gen. **1**.10, 12, 25, 31, etc.)?

3. Note the stress on the creative word in Gen. **1** and **2**. What implications may be drawn from this (cf. John **1**.1 ff.; Col. **1**.15 f.; Heb. **1**.1 f.)?

4. Can we learn anything of significance for our prayer-life from Job's outspoken complaint (**10**.8–22, cf. Jer. **4**.10; **12**.1–5; **15**.15–21)?

5. What should be our attitude to the material world (see note on Job **38**.1–38, cf. Matt. **6**.25–33)?

6. Discuss fully some of the issues raised in the note on Job **38**.39–**39**.30.

TWO

Implications

9 : Glory !

Psalm 29

In the O.T., God is depicted as unique, but not solitary. Here the 'heavenly beings' (1) are invited to worship Him, as elsewhere individual man may do so (Psa. 103.1; 104.1). The fact that God is often noted as surrounded by the hosts of angels (cf. 1 Kings 22.19; Job 1.6; 38.7; Pss. 82.1; 89.7; Isa. 6.2) does not obscure His monotheism but rather enhances it; in this assemblage He is apart, the object of unqualified adoration.

God revealed Himself in the O.T. period in three major ways : by direct revelation to man; by His sovereign acts in history; and by His acts in nature. The third, which underlines the cosmic element in revelation (this is His world, and He controls it), is prominent in this psalm. There is an artistry, an awesome majesty, in this description of a thunderstorm, pictured as coming in from the Mediterranean (3), spending its full fury upon the wooded, mountainous region of Lebanon and Hermon (5 f., Sirion is the Phoenician name for Hermon), and disappearing southward into the wilderness of Kadesh (8). The sevenfold 'the voice of the Lord' gives a vivid impression of the deep rumbling of the thunder-claps, which causes the apparently-immovable mountains to tremble. The purpose of the psalmist was not to show God as a 'nature-god', but to use this awe-inspiring aspect of His creation to convey an impression of His majesty. A thunderstorm can create terror and leave behind a wake of destruction (9a), but

16

the awareness of the Divine majesty is so dominating that His creation can but exclaim 'Glory' (9b).

In v. 10 there may be an allusion to the pagan mythology of the primeval victory over the forces of chaos (cf. Psa. **77**.16 ff.) and to the ceremony, linked with these beliefs amongst Israel's neighbours, of the annual death, resurrection and subsequent enthronement of the god, symbolized in the person of his representative, the king. But the God of Israel is not thus to be identified or described. He never has the power of His rule taken away, He 'sits enthroned as king for ever', without rivals. Those who speak of monotheism emerging late in Israel overlook the significance of such allusions.

The supreme greatness of God, however, does not mean that He is remote from His people's every-day concerns; indeed His very omnipotence encourages them to turn to Him in intercession (11). The God who is infinitely greater than the thunderstorm is the One who can give strength and peace to those who adore and trust Him.

10 : 'The Earth is the Lord's . . .'

Psalm 104

A. Weiser comments on this psalm, 'The relation of this nature-hymn to the story of creation in the first chapters of Genesis is like that of a coloured picture to the clear lines of a woodcut.' The simplicity of the Genesis narrative is here filled out with warmth of sympathy, depth of understanding and reverence of spirit. In Psa. **29**.1 the heavenly hosts were invited to worship God. Here it is a humble, individual man whose spirit soars upward in adoration as he discerns beauty as well as order and purpose, and praises the sheer glory as well as the wisdom of the Creator. That God not only creates but sustains all things fills him with a deep sense of awe, and he responds in trust. It is possibly one of our losses as evangelical Christians that, in our necessary stress on the moral aspects of this universe, we have lost some of the joy and exuberance that result from meeting God at this cosmic level.

17

The O.T. has no abstract view of nature. This world originated in God, it was God-centred and God-sustained. In the picture of the structure of the world (2 f., 5), in the terms used to describe Him (3b, the Canaanite god, Baal, is frequently described as 'the Rider of the Clouds') and in His victory over the seas, symbol of the forces of chaos (6–9), there are again links with the world-view of the surrounding nations. But they are no more than allusions. Israel's view of the Creator is consistently distinct and uncompromised.

We find elements in this psalm that we have noted before. In sublime word-pictures the psalmist shows the riches of God's provision for all His creatures, including the remotest (18). Time, in the ordering of day and night, subserves His will and allows for the diverse activities of the wild beasts and man (19–23). He is the great Universal Provider (27 f.), and the issues of death, as well as life, are firmly in His control (29). There is a resurrecting power in the activity of His Spirit (30) and the more spectacular aspects of nature proceed from Him (32) as well as the beneficent features already observed. In the light of this exalted conception the psalmist deplores the very existence of those who flaunt God's rule (35), they are an affront to His majesty. For his own part, his spirit flows out to God in a torrent of praise that he could wish was eternal (33 f., 35b).

The Prophetic Vision

11 : The Future is His Also

Isaiah 11

If God be the Sovereign Creator and Sustainer of all things as well as the Lord of History, then He must control future events. We are indebted to the great prophets who saw clearly this purpose in history and worked out its implications, not only for Israel, but for the whole world. Amos, who preceded Isaiah, foretold the climax of history in the 'Day of the Lord' (e.g. 5.18 ff.; 8.9–14; 9.11–15), but it was Isaiah who gave shape and content to this eschatological hope. This prophecy probably dates from the reign of the apostate King Ahaz (735–715 B.C.), when Judah was in the iron grip of Assyria. Some scholars have suggested that it was originally a coronation-oracle, possibly for the accession of Hezekiah, the son of Ahaz, but vs. 9 f. point far beyond any ruler of Judah. Moreover the opening verse suggests something unexpected, a new beginning following the rejection of the present line of Davidic kings (cf. Mic. **5**.1 f.; Isa. **53**.2). Jeremiah, a century later than Isaiah, announced the name of this 'righteous Branch' as 'The Lord is our Righteousness' (**23**.5 f.). Such passages as these, in which an individual figure, the agent of God's salvation, is prominent, are properly called Messianic.

The transformation of the world scene contrasts with the catastrophic end of the great world-power of Assyria (**10**.33 f.). It will embrace the animal kingdom and will result in a restoration of creation's harmony (6–9). Paradise will be restored and the evil effects of man's sin reversed (cf. Gen. **3**.14–19). There is a poetic element here, but it must not be dismissed as allegory. Paul teaches a similar truth in Rom. **8**.19–22. The centuries-old breach between Israel (Ephraim) and Judah will be healed (12 f.). This decisive intervention of God will inevitably involve judgement upon the heathen nations (e.g. 14 f.), but the purpose is not to exalt Israel as the central world power, but to bring all nations to 'the knowledge of the Lord' (9). Later Judaism was to lose sight of this distinction. Do not overlook the qualities of the future Messiah (3–5). These reflect the nature of God's rule and ought to characterize His people. The place of the Spirit of the Lord (2), both in connection with the Messiah Himself and with the establishment of His Kingdom, is further stressed in Isa. **32**.15; **42**.1 (cf. Matt. **12**.18–21; Luke **4**.18 f.) and Joel **2**.28 f. The latter part of this chapter (11–16) received a partial fulfilment in the return of the exiles from captivity in 538 B.C.

Notice the relevance of the psalm of praise (Isa. **12**) immediately after this prophecy, affirming the final establishment of the Messianic Kingdom. Nothing can thwart God's purposes!

12 : The Incomparable

Isaiah 40

This chapter illustrates the practical nature of O.T. theology, although the view of God depicted here is so incomparably sublime that it can only be described as 'pure monotheism'. Isaiah demonstrates the majesty of God to shake the Jews from their apathetic self-pity, and to encourage them to act on His promise in returning to Jerusalem. The key verse is v. 27 which reproaches the nation for suggesting God's indifference to their misfortune.

First there is the announcement of the end of the exile (1 f.). Then God is shown as the great King, leading His people in His royal progress across the miles between Babylonia and Zion (3 ff.), in fulfilment of the prophetic word (e.g. Jer. **25**.11 f.; **29**.10–14). Man, like grass and the flowers, is frail, but God's word is sure. So, long before the party had set out from Babylonia, the prophet pictures its *arrival* in Jerusalem, where the herald excitedly proclaims the good news (9 ff.). The magnificent combination of God's strength and tenderness as the King-Shepherd reminds us that these were the qualities required of an earthly ruler and the Messiah (e.g. 2 Sam. **5**.2; Psa. **78**.70 ff.; Jer. **23**.3–6; Ezek. **34**.22 ff.; **37**.24; cf. Psa. **23**).

Then follows a section which, in a series of vivid pictures, shows just how great God is and how immeasurable the gulf between Him and man (12–26). This world, and even the universe itself, seem vast to man but are infinitesimal when compared with their Creator (12 ff., cf. v. 22). The nations, including mighty Babylonia which had laid its cruel yoke upon Judah, were equally insignificant (15 ff., cf. v. 23). Man, pathetically blind, might worship the gods of his own construction (18 ff.), or the stars (25 f.), but this was an insult to Him who created and ordered the heavenly host. Lord of History as well as Creation, He was unique and man could safely trust in Him; indeed, not to do so was utterly unreasonable. This truth remains unchanged; the nations, with all their bravado, are still 'like a drop from a bucket'. Spiritual victory is available to all who, like Israel of old, are in covenant-relationship with this incomparable God (28–31). Whatever the circumstances, His unlimited power is available to those who wait upon Him (31, cf. **64**.4).

13 : Worthy of Praise

Isaiah 44.9–28

When Israel's faith could properly be described as mono-theistic is disputed. In the Mosaic period Israel's God is so great in His saving acts that all rivals are eclipsed, yet many theologians, somewhat unreasonably, deny the word monotheism to this period since there is no formal denial that other gods exist. Amos, likewise, shows both the sovereignty and the care which God extends to other nations (e.g. 1.3–2.3; 9.7), demonstrating again a preoccupation with the great, active attributes which make Him unrivalled. But idolatry had its attractions. It was easier to worship some-thing that could be seen than the unseen Creator. Isaiah, in his thoroughgoing attempt to show that Israel's God is unique, now develops the thoughts before expressed (e.g. 40.18 ff.; 41.6 f., 29) and moves into a full-scale attack on idolatry (9–20). With the exception of Jer. 10.1–16, nowhere else in the O.T. is there such a withering, satirical onslaught, demon-strating the utter stupidity of idol worship.

Against this background of impotence and futility the true God stands forth in splendid isolation and majesty (21–23). His elective-grace is shown in His choice of Israel (21, 24a). Israel is His servant. This title denotes the responsibility and privilege of an office held. The servant stands in an intimate yet subordinate relationship to his Master. Yahweh is also the God of redemption (22 ff.). Here the thought goes beyond a physical deliverance from captivity; it is a moral deliverance from sin and transgression. The picture of v. 22 is particularly appropriate to Palestine where the early morning cloud or mist is quickly dispelled by the rising sun (cf. Mal. 4.2; Luke 1.78 f.). The series of questions—for this is what they are—in vs. 24–28 all requires the answer, 'No one but You, Lord'.

In v. 26 the tone becomes prophetical. The rebuilding of Jerusalem, the other devastated cities and the Temple, was the necessary attestation to the surrounding nations that Yahweh was sovereign, and working for His people. Even more remarkable was His use of Cyrus, the Persian king, the great world-figure of his age (28, 45.1–6, cf. 10.5–19). Unbe-known to Cyrus (45.4b) he was fulfilling the role of the shep-herd to God's people, a prophecy uniquely fulfilled (cf.

21

Ezra **1**). No wonder the prophet calls upon the heights and depths and all nature to praise such a God (23)!

14 : God is Real

Amos 4.4–13; 9.1–6

Since God is both Sovereign and Righteous, and the absolute Lord of Creation, it is to be expected that He will correct or punish His people when they sin. Amos has much to say about the social injustice prevalent in Israel c. 750 B.C. (e.g. **2**.6 ff.; **5**.10–13; **8**.4 ff.), but the immediate context is the religious hypocrisy of the sanctuaries (**4**.4 f., cf. **5**.4 f.). There was scrupulous attention to religious detail but it was for their own gratification, and completely unacceptable to God (cf. ·**5**.21–24). Israel, therefore, was visited with a series of 'natural catastrophes'; famine (6), drought (7 f.), plant diseases and the ravages of locusts (9), plague (10, the low-lying, irrigated delta of Egypt was a notorious plague-area, cf. Deut. **7**.15; **28**.27) and earthquake (11, cf. **1**.1) followed each other in succession. God also used the power of Israel's enemies (10), showing that He was Lord of History as well as Nature. Israelites ought to have discerned the chastening hand of God in this, and realized that His purpose was to bring them back to Himself, as the fivefold chorus 'yet you did not return to me' indicates. There were love and grace as well as righteous judgement in His actions (cf. Heb. **12**.5 ff.). But it was all in vain. Israel was insensitive to God, and His chastening rod was to be set aside for a more decisive judgement (12). The nature of this is not specified, and is therefore the more fearsome, but it involved a direct confrontation with God Himself (cf. Heb. **10**.30 f.).

In vision Amos saw the outworking of this final judgement (**9**.1–4). It began in the temple of Bethel, which, instead of being a fountain of blessing, was itself a source of corruption (cf. 3.14). The picture is of an earthquake followed by an invasion. There will be no way of escape, for God's power extends to Sheol, heaven, the mountain-top, the ocean depths, even the prisoner-of-war camp! There is a fearful contrast between the imagery of Psa. 139.7–12 and our passage; in one

22

there is the pursuit of love, in the other the inexorable pursuit of judgement. Similarly, 'I will set my eyes upon them for evil' (4) contrasts with the tender, watchful gaze of Psa. **34.15.** The point of both sets of contrasts, however, is that God is a *real* God, not to be treated lightly as He was by Israel, or ignored. Notice how the two doxologies (**4.13; 9.5 f.**) contribute to this picture of an active, transcendent God.

Questions and themes for study and discussion on Studies 9-14

1. In what ways can we see the glory of God in nature? Is such knowledge of God sufficient?

2. Consider the relationship between the created and the Creator (Psa. **104**).

3. What may we learn of Jesus Christ from Isa. **11** (cf. **9.1–7**)?

4. Consider the relationship of theology to the details of the everyday life (cf. note on Isa. **40**).

5. Does God still control the great world powers, and their rulers, as He did Cyrus (Isa. **44.28**, etc.)?

6. If God is as Amos (**4.4–13; 9.1–6**, etc.) describes Him, do we take Him seriously enough?

23

THREE

Christ as Lord of Creation

15 : 'The First of His Signs'

John 2.1–12

Christ's first miracle has been criticized for its apparently unnecessary extravagance, and because it wrought no lasting benefit. Such an attitude is unwarranted. The key to its understanding lies in the fact that it was 'the first of his signs' (11). The importance of a 'sign', in the context of Christ's ministry, lies in what it *signifies* rather than in the event itself. Bear in mind also that this particular sign was limited to a select few; the mother and disciples of our Lord and a few servants. Even the steward of the feast was unaware that a miracle had taken place (9 f.). Unlike most of our Lord's signs, this has no recorded explanation, although its effect on the disciples gives us a significant clue (11). The following points are relevant:

1. Christ, noted in 1.3 as the active Agent in creation, is set forth as the Lord of Creation, with power to transform the more mundane elements into something richer.

2. As in the O.T. revelation of God the Father, this sovereign power of the Son is available too in response to human faith, here that of Mary herself (5). His main purpose in coming into the world was to redeem it, but a sympathetic concern and active involvement with humanity characterized Him as He moved purposefully to His goal (cf. Heb. 4.14 ff.). Notice how the way of happiness, here the avoidance of embarrassment to the steward of the feast and shame to the bridal couple, lay in full obedience to His commands (5 ff.).

24

This has a remarkable similarity to the O.T. teaching (e.g. Deut. **30**.20; Prov. **3**.5–8).

3. The reference of Christ to His 'hour' (4) has throughout the Gospels a connection with His final passion. It is likely that Mary imagined that one dramatic miracle would set Him forth clearly as the Messiah. Jesus points out that this unveiling is still in the future—for Him, of course, at Calvary —yet there *is* a revelation to His disciples (11). Possibly this incident convinced them of His divine origin (**1**.51) and marked Him out as 'the Lamb of God' (**1**.29, 36). Disciple-ship for them was henceforth a relationship of personal faith.

4. The explanation given in v. 6 is surely not incidental. The miracle was a parable of Judaism's inadequacy and of the richer, fuller contribution Christ was to make. When human resources fail, God's intervention can bring lasting satisfaction, even salvation! The wine, then, was the symbol of the gospel of grace and of the full provision He would make at the climax of His ministry when His hour had fully come.

16 : The Claim of Equality

John 5.1–18

From the revelation to His disciples of Christ's Lordship (**2**.11) John now documents the events that brought Him into conflict with the Jewish religious authorities (cf. Mark **2**.1— **3**.6). This revelation takes four aspects in today's portion:

1. Christ shows Himself as the Lord of Life by His power to heal (2–9). The helplessness of this man, and his apparent apathy are stressed, but no human situation is beyond the power of the Lord of Life. The 'feast' (1) was probably Purim, celebrated in March.

2. Christ shows His Lordship over the Sabbath and, there-fore, His superiority over the Law. The Law of the Sabbath (e.g. Exod. **23**.12; Jer. **17**.21 f.) as interpreted in Jewish tradition was frequently attacked by our Lord, since it so misrepresented the Divine purpose (cf. Matt. **12**.1–14; Luke **13**.10–17; **14**.1–6). The rabbinic law declared that if a man wilfully carried anything from a public place to a private

home on the Sabbath he was to die. The healed man, therefore took a great risk, but in obeying his Healer, he was responding to One with ultimate authority. The point which Jesus makes in v. 17 is that God's Sabbath-rest does not mean inactivity. Just as it is the nature of light to shine so it is God's nature to continue His unceasing, sustaining care of this universe. The implication is that the Sabbath is to be observed positively, in what glorifies God and furthers His will, rather than negatively (cf. Isa. 58.13 f.).

3. Christ shows concern for and authority over sin (14). The implication is that this man's infirmity was the result of sin (cf. Mark 2.5–11).

4. Christ claims equality with God (18). His work of healing on the Sabbath, He asserts, was complementary to, and a continuation of, the Father's work. The remainder of the chapter (19–47) amplifies this statement; in the perfect Father-Son relationship He cannot but fulfil the Father's will. It was this claim to a unique Sonship, rather than one shared with all men, which so isolated Jesus from others. Only One equal with God could deal with His laws as Jesus had done. This claim the Jews rejected, and the persecution of v. 16 now sharpens (18). The issue of Christ's claim to be the Incarnate God still divides men. Is your response one of faith or rejection?

17: 'The Resurrection and the Life'

John 11.1–44

The raising of Lazarus was the last and greatest sign which John records. The deity of Christ is perfectly revealed in this incident, which showed His sovereignty over death itself. Twice before Christ had demonstrated His power to restore life: in the cases of Jairus' daughter (Mark 5.35–43) and the widow of Nain's son (Luke 7.11–17). In each of these it could have been claimed by our Lord's enemies that it was a state of coma, not death. But Lazarus, when raised, had been dead for four days, and the physical evidence of death, in the putrefaction of the corpse, had set in (39). We may link with this the Jewish tradition that a man's spirit hovered in the vicinity of the tomb until the third day, when it finally went away. Lazarus was dead, of that there was no doubt. In the hopelessness of his condition, and the grief of the sisters, there was epitomized the dread fact that man's sin brought death. But behind sin there was the work of the evil one, and death, called 'the last enemy' in 1 Cor. **15**.26, was the final evidence of his power. It was surely this fact that so deeply agitated Christ (33), and it was this realm that Christ invaded in this miracle, for He alone can effect the transformation from corruption into incorruption, from mortality into immortality (1 Cor. **15**.42 ff.). We also perceive a symbol of His own decisive victory over sin, death and the grave.

Notice the blending of our Lord's perfect humanity, witnessed in His tears (35), and His divinity, illustrated by His knowledge of the death of Lazarus (14). Notice, too, the evidence of complete unity between the Father and the Son. Martha was aware of this (22), and our Lord's prayer also reveals it (41 f.). One important practical point emerges (39). Christ could easily have removed the stone Himself, but He limits the exercise of His supernatural power, and allows man to co-operate with Him in so far as he is able. The conversation with Martha is of crucial theological importance (21-27). She may have thought Jesus was simply echoing a conventional platitude (23 f.) but He encourages her to faith in Himself as the Source of true spiritual life. Whoever is in that personal relationship of faith *has* life, in Him, as a present, permanent possession. Death cannot destroy or even interrupt this. The believer lives on through death, and the resurrection is the inevitable consequence of life in Christ. God declares in righteousness 'the soul that sins shall die' (Ezek. **18**.4, cf. Jer. **31**.30), But the word of the Son of God, restoring man to communion with the Father, is 'whoever lives and believes in me shall never die'.

18 : He knows !

Matthew 6.25-34

The key to this section is the phrase 'your heavenly Father' (26, 32). To Him we have access, in prayer. Such access opens for us His treasury (cf. v. 6). Notice how our Lord builds up to this section by advocating sincerity and integrity (16 ff.), a sense of true values (19 ff.), a correct vision or perspective (22 f.) and singlemindedness (24). Anxious, fretting care, which concentrates fussily on earthly and selfish concerns and distracts attention from God, is diametrically opposed to these. Christ gives three reasons why we should avoid such a state of heart:

1. God, as Creator, fashioned our bodies and gave us life (25). Surely, then, He will provide for the food and clothing necessary to sustain what He has created! The lesser things are implied in the greater.

2. God, in His providential care, provides for the humbler creatures of His kingdom (26). Will He do less for man, the crown of His creation?

3. God is prodigal in His beautification of this world (28 ff.). Each flower, so exquisite in beauty and perfect in design, and yet so transient, surpasses the splendour of a Solomon. Man can trust such a God to provide adequately for those with whom He has personal communion. Notice here our Lord's evident love of nature.

Worry, in such a context, is both useless (27), and characteristic of the godless who have no knowledge of a Heavenly Father (32). We should trust Him, therefore, and see our worries in the perspective of a world where He is supreme. Man is not merely a creature requiring simply to be fed and clothed. He has higher concerns, to please God and to glorify Him by seeking the extension of His kingly rule (33). God will provide richly for men when they display such an attitude (cf. the order of the petitions in vs. 10 f.).

Verse 34 does not contradict the remainder of the section. Each day does bring its quota of difficulties but these do not destroy the peace of the man who knows God as his Heavenly Father. But we have to deal with the *present* not the unknown future, so that anxious scheming which destroys peace of mind is to be avoided. He is the eternal God, and tomorrow, when it comes, will find Him still in control and adequately prepared.

Apostolic Reference Points

19 : The Great Turning-Point

Acts 14.8–18; 17.22–34

These sections contain the two examples of Paul's preaching to wholly heathen groups—at Lystra and Athens. His exposition was firmly based on the O.T. revelation, although he did not quote directly, in deference to his Gentile listeners. Since the fuller discussion comes in the Areopagus address, we will make that the foundation of our study.

Paul begins with the Athenian's tacit admission of their ignorance in the erection of an altar to 'an unknown god' (17.23). The very multiplicity of their altars shows that they have no real conception of the nature of the one true God. Similarly, at Lystra, there is a contrast between 'these vain things' (a standard way of describing the heathen idols in the O.T., cf. Jer. 2.5) and the 'living God' (14.15). Paul depicts God as the sole Creator and universal Lord (17.24) and the bountiful Provider (14.17). He cannot be confined within a man-made shrine and thus brought under man's control (17.24, cf. 1 Kings 8.27), nor is He dependent on man's worship, although He desires the true worship of the human heart (17.25a, cf. Pss. 50.7–15; 96.9). As the Originator and Sustainer of life (17.25b) He is perfectly self-sufficient. The universal brotherhood of man (17.26) is complemented by His assertion of the Universal Fatherhood (17.29)—in terms of His responsibility for the existence of all—in a way reminiscent of Amos 9.7. All this may be described as 'natural revelation', which we will consider more fully in Rom. 1.16–32. The point which Paul makes at both Lystra and Athens is that idolatry is incompatible with what may reasonably be known of God in the natural realm. Man ought at least to worship Him as Creator and recognize His rich provision. Even the Gentile poets acknowledged the relationship between man and the Deity (17.28), therefore man demeans himself when he worships what he has himself fashioned (17.29).

Such 'ignorance' has been made unpardonable in the light of the full revelation of God in Christ (17.30, cf. 14.16; Rom. 3.25). Paul saw the fact of Christ as the great watershed in history, the touch-stone by which men are judged (cf. John 5.27). His thought in both passages is highly compressed, but we see clearly that for him Christ's coming ended the period of ignorance concerning God's nature. This new knowledge is not conceived as merely intellectual, it is moral and spiritual, leading men to repentance (17.30).

One practical point emerges from the superstitious attitudes of the men of Lystra. They believed that their work of healing showed Paul and Barnabas to be gods. In this they were mistaken, for the source of power was in God, not in these men themselves, but it is a fact that we reveal God in what we, His servants, accomplish in His will.

20 : Good News Indeed !

Romans 1.16–32

Paul deals here with the same theme that he had expounded at Lystra and Athens, i.e. the fact of a general revelation of God, but at a much greater depth. He affirms that man, in the likeness of God and endowed with personality and conscience, is able to discern an individual, powerful Being who created all things (19 f.) and whom he ought to worship and honour (21). Moreover, since God's essential goodness is revealed in the richness of His provision, man ought to 'give thanks to him' (21).

Man's fall from grace was not due to ignorance but to wilful rejection. He is culpable, deliberately suppressing a knowledge of God (18 f., 21, 25). Because of this all his attitudes and values are distorted. God was dethroned and man, in his pride, became his own arbiter, human reason supplanting the God-given revelation (21 f.). The consequence was idolatry, which reflected man's debased standards (23). The inevitable accompaniment of this repudiation of a supreme, moral Being was the descent into all kinds of vice (24–31). This in itself was a punishment, and when we add the consequences of this kind of life upon the individual, the family and society generally we see a strong element of justice, noted in the three-fold 'God gave them up' (24, 26, 28). The expression indicates a judicial act expressing God's rule over this world, into the constitution of which He has woven His moral law. Those who sow to the flesh reap a fearful harvest of corruption (Gal. **6**.7, cf. **5**.16–24; Rom. **8**.6 ff.). It is clear that Paul views mankind generally as coming under the wrath of God (18, cf. **3**.9–20), although he allows the possibility of some Gentiles being responsive to the limited light which comes to them by natural revelation, apart from the Jewish Law (**2**.14 ff., note that the standard by which they are judged, or justified, is still 'Christ Jesus').

Against this sombre background Paul's unashamed declaration of the gospel of Christ comes with the ring of hope to despairing men (16 f.). A totally new and complete revelation of God, it has power to undo all the evil wrought by sin. The 'righteousness of God' (17, note the frequency of the phrase in this epistle) is a quality unattainable by unaided man (**3**.10), even by the Jew, diligent in his attention to the Law (cf. Paul's own testimony in ch. **7**). But God, by His gracious saving activity through His Son, has brought it within man's range (Isa. **45**.23 f.; **51**.4 f.). Man receives it by faith (17) and henceforth the 'righteousness of God' is to characterize his conduct (**6**.13, 18 f.). No wonder Paul concludes the doctrinal section of this epistle with an outburst of praise to the God who can so transform a situation (**11**.33–36)!

21 : The Self and Society

1 Corinthians 6.12–20; 8.1–13

Doctrine must be related to everyday behaviour or else it becomes a meaningless abstraction. The Christian has been brought back from the realm of sin into an effective fellowship with God, a union made possible at infinite cost (**6**.20). This leads to:

1. A regard for self (**6**.12–20). 'All things are lawful for me' (12, cf. **10**.23) was obviously a catch-phrase of the Corinthians, meaning virtually, 'I can do what I like'. Paul denies this; a Christian must not do anything which would be hurtful to his true self, or which would dominate him. His teaching concerning the body is of great significance. The Christian is united to the Lord, a part of His body (13b, 15, 17) and this is not merely a spirit or soul relationship. So exalted is Paul's view that he does not hesitate to describe the body as 'a

temple', indwelt by the Holy Spirit (19). This brings an obligation to glorify Him in our bodies. Two things which could militate against this are touched upon. The first is gluttony, the attitude that eating and drinking are the supreme end in life (13). Paul shows the folly of such a policy, declaring both food and the digestive organs themselves to be perishable. Of greater consequence is sexual immorality, which is incompatible with Christianity since it takes what is united to Christ and gives it away to another (15 ff.). Sexual perversion is the very antithesis of the Lordship of Christ.

2. A regard for others (8.1–13). A Christian is a member of a society, which will invariably be imperfect—that at Corinth was idolatrous and corrupt. In particular, meat originally offered to idols was both plentiful and cheap (cf. **10**.23–33) and posed an acute problem for the Corinthian Christians. Should they eat meat from this source or not? It is stressed that, since there is only one God, an idol has no objective existence (4 ff.). Moreover the meat offered to non-existent idols is part of His provision for mankind, to be enjoyed, although again Paul stresses that eating is an incidental function (8). He then advocates freedom in this area (cf. the stricter attitude of the Jerusalem believers, Acts **15**.29). But freedom was not unlimited, for intellectual discernment must never outrun love. At Corinth there were those duller intellects who still attached significance to idols and whose consciences were tender on this issue. The stronger brethren with 'knowledge' were riding roughshod over their weaker brethren. Circumstances have changed but the Pauline principle remains. Our dealings with any other Christian must be on the highest possible level, for he is 'the brother for whom Christ died' (11). Failure to do this not only hurts the weaker brother, it is a positive sin against Christ (12). In a fundamental sense I am my brother's keeper (13).

22 : The Pre-Eminent Christ

Colossians 1.15–23

A cardinal rule in Bible study is that a verse, section or chapter should be viewed in relationship to its context. The letter to the Colossians was prompted by Paul's contact with

Epaphras (**1.**7 f.; **4.**12 f.) who had given him a generally-encouraging report, but spoke of a local heresy (a form of Judaistic Gnosticism) which was troubling the church. Paul outlines some aspects of this false belief in **2.**8–23; it denied Christ His rightful place by laying stress on angelic intermediaries (**2.**18) and by insisting on the necessity of certain legalistic, ascetic practices. Paul deals with this problem in what H. C. G. Moule described as 'The Creed of Christ's Pre-eminence' (**1.**15–20). But this is no mere polemic, it is a hymn of adoration which places Christ in the centre of faith and revelation. Paul notes :

1. Christ's relationship to God (15). 'Image' has the sense of 'manifestation or likeness revealed' (cf. John **1.**18; 2 Cor. **4.**6; Heb. **1.**3). 'The first-born of all creation' cannot mean that Christ was the first act of creation (cf. v. 17), but rather, as is linguistically possible, 'the one prior to creation', cf. Moffatt's translation 'born first before all the creation'.

2. Christ's relationship to Creation (16). The Gnostic heresy which stressed the function of angelic intermediaries also held that matter was essentially evil, and that the Highest God could have no contact with it. But Paul affirms that Christ was the sole Creator, the Lord of the Universe and of History. Moreover, He is the One who gives significance and coherence to creation. All this sets Christ apart in unrivalled splendour.

3. Christ's relationship to the Church (18). Again, as the 'pioneer and perfecter of our faith' (Heb. **12.**2), He is absolute Lord, the figure of the body hinting at the interdependence of the members (cf. Eph. **4.**15 f.).

4. The completeness of Christ's Work (20–23). This is asserted first in a general way (20). Notice how Paul's thought of redemption includes the material creation (cf. Rom. **8.**19–22). Then Paul sharpens his focus upon the Colossians themselves (21–23). Christ's redemptive work must not be viewed abstractly; it must be related to the individual (cf. Gal. **2.**20). Following hard upon Paul's insistence on the full deity of Christ the phrase 'his body of flesh by his death' (22), which implies His full humanity, is of vital importance. Again, the Gnostic heretics would find the thought of the Supreme Being dying repugnant, and 'flesh' was a 'dirty word' in their circles. But Paul is uncompromising in his statement that Christ was both fully God and fully man.

FOUR

God and History in the Psalter

23 : Universal Praise

Psalm 103

There are certain psalms which are universal favourites because they witness to what is basic in our relationship with God. Psa. 103 typifies the highest O.T. piety, with its focus upon the sheer, unmerited grace of God contrasting with man's inherent frailty and sinfulness. The key phrase is undoubtedly God's 'steadfast love' (4, 8, 11, 17, Heb. *chesed*) which has an intimate association with the covenant relationship (cf. v. 18). Elsewhere we find reference to the *chesed* of man in the covenant bond, i.e. his filial loyalty and obedience to the Lord (e.g. Hos. **6**.6, cf. Mic. **6**.8), and since man is also related to man in the covenant bond, *chesed*, i.e. brotherly-love, has an important place (e.g. Hos. **4**.1; **12**.6). But here the attention is concentrated on God's *chesed*, i.e. His faithfulness and unmerited love.

1. God and the individual (1–5). The sense of gratitude to a gracious and merciful God is so strong that the psalmist's heart is uplifted in total response (1 f.). There is an obvious background of personal sin, possibly connected with adversity, which demonstrates that the psalmist takes seriously God's righteousness and judgement. But He is a saving God whose delivering grace reaches down to the individual. One of the most remarkable features of the psalmists was the way they brought the whole might and grace of God to bear on their particular situation. God was not simply concerned with nations or communities, nor did He dole out His grace in

minute portions. David saw also that this saving and renewing activity reached forward into the limitless future (5).

2. God and the nation (6–18). Modern scholars use the expression 'Salvation-history' to describe the unbroken series of God's acts on behalf of His people, reaching back to the Mosaic period (7, cf. Exod. **34**.6 f.). The patient, limitless forbearance of God so beautifully described (8–14) is amply revealed in the chequered history of wayward Israel. Notice again how sin is taken seriously (10, cf. Psa. **130**.3 f.). Indeed, man's sin and frailty (14 ff.) appear as an immense gulf between the Creator and His creation, but God, in His covenant grace, has bridged the abyss and removed the sin which shatters the personal relationship with Him (Isa. **59**.2). But redeemed Israel is to make the response of loyal obedience (18).

3. God and the Universe (19–22). David, recognizing the universal sovereignty of Yahweh, calls upon the entire heavenly host to join in the chorus. But amid the supra-terrestrial paean of praise, his own small voice still sounds forth bravely (22b)!

24 : The Present Reality

Psalm 105

We observed the general principles of the Lord's dealings with Israel in Psa. **103**. Today's psalm is more specific, and traces the hand of the Lord over a well-defined period of time, viz. from the promise to the patriarchs (8–11) until its fulfilment in the possession of the promised land (44). This is much more than a history lesson; the Lord Himself is the subject of almost every verb and it is His grace, and His faithfulness to His word, which are emphasized. No author is mentioned but a comparison with 1 Chron. **16**.7–36, which also incorporates Pss. **96**; **106**.47 f., shows that it was written or commissioned by David himself when the ark was brought up to Jerusalem. Possibly it was recited annually at the anniversary of this event and made the occasion of a renewal of the covenant (notice the stress in vs. 8–11). The covenant in Israel was not regarded as simply a fact of history. It had present implications and each successive generation entered into it by a personal response and participation (8). In this way the saving acts of God became present realities, and the annual covenant-renewal became the occasion of remembrance, joy and assurance of future strength (1–6). An understanding of this helps us to appreciate the significance of other recitals of the Salvation-history of Israel, usually associated with some significant national occasion (e.g. Neh. **9**.6–38). God is *always* mindful of His people, His attitude towards them remains gracious and protective. He is a *present* Reality, whose goodness is always manifested before He outlines His requirements (45).

The survey of history demonstrates God's control: the seeming insignificance of the patriarchal period (12–15, cf. Deut. **26**.5–9); the successive misfortunes of Joseph (16–22); the confrontation in Egypt (23–38), the requirements of the wilderness period (39 f.), all these showed His almighty power to overrule. He has not lost this power or graciousness in His dealings with the spiritual Israel in the new covenantal relationship!

25 : Learning from Experience

Psalm 106

There is a marked contrast between the spirit and standpoint of this psalm and its predecessor. Psa. **105**, composed in the early period of the monarchy, is characterized by a certain optimism; Psa. **106** is virtually a confession of national guilt and weakness. One of the reasons for this is that it was composed much later. Verse 47 almost certainly indicates a date after the destruction of Jerusalem and the beginning of the Exile in 587 B.C. The viewpoint is similar to that of the historical books, Joshua—Kings, whose editors show the effects of sin and apostasy upon Israel, and the Lord's control of history to chastise His people. In a survey from the Exodus to the Exile, the psalmist shows that Israel was always completely undeserving of the divine grace, and invariably unbelieving, rebellious and ungrateful. The ideal, noted in v. 3, was *never* realized. But Pss. **105** and **106** have one important point in common: they both high-light the Lord's unfailing grace and steadfast love (1 f., 7, 45). In Psa. **106** this is in spite of the provocation of a guilty nation over long centuries. The point underscored heavily is the almost unbelievable faithfulness of God within the covenant-relationship. This long-suffering attitude must not be construed as weakness, however, as the righteous judgements of God are also clearly detailed.

The marked interest in acts of religious disobedience (19 f., 28, 36–39) probably indicates the cultic setting of this psalm. The worshipping individual does not detach himself from this confession of national waywardness and set himself up as a judge upon past generations. He admits that he and his fellows are in the same condemnation (6). A previous generation had blamed its misfortunes upon its forefathers, and opted out of responsibility, an attitude condemned and corrected by Jeremiah and Ezekiel (cf. Jer. **31**.29 f.; Ezek. **18**). But now the psalmist, and indeed the whole congregation, accept their own moral and spiritual responsibility. They, as much as their ancestors, stand in need of the Lord's gracious forbearance. So the psalm concludes with a prayer for a miracle comparable with the Exodus (47) and then with a great doxology (48). God is *still* able to deliver, His saving acts are not relegated to the realm of ancient history.

God and the Nation

26 : The First Step

Genesis 12.1–20

After the amazingly compressed detail of Gen. **1–11** a leisureliness and a wealth of incidental information come into the narrative as the great drama of God's redemptive activity begins, significantly, with the divine word of challenge and promise. Since God is God, this word is certain of fulfilment and the fulfilment itself becomes one of the proofs of Yahweh's deity—no other god has ever announced beforehand a programme so miraculously completed (cf. Isa. **43**.12; **44**.7 f.; **45**.21 and especially **55**.11).

But the response of faith to the divine initiative is scarcely less remarkable. Abraham left the familiar for a completely unknown destination (Heb. 11.8); he found the promised territory already occupied (6b); his legal right to the land was non-existent; indeed, the only territory he could ever claim as his own was a burial ground (Gen. 23.17–20). The lack of an heir seemed another impediment to the fulfilment of the divine promise. Yet Abraham's faith scarcely wavered, although the incident in Egypt (10–20), where he appears to have gone on his own initiative, could have endangered God's plan. God's power was revealed in the realms of nature (the plagues of v. 17) and history (His use of Pharaoh) to bring Abraham back to the promised land. While the major emphasis is on the sovereign act of God's choice, in line with His purpose of universal redemption, we should not overlook the . reality of personal communion between God and Abraham, which the latter expressed in obedience (4) and worship (7 f.). Verse 7 anticipates the detailed covenant of 15.18–21.

In the light of Israel's subsequent history it is important to observe that the promise was spiritual and universalistic, not narrowly nationalistic (2 f.). In spite of the restrictive Judaism which emerged at times in later centuries, the realization that God's purposes were not restricted was never completely obliterated. The promise itself was remembered (18.18; 22.18; 26.4; 28.14; Jer. 4.2); Israel's priestly, mediating ministry was affirmed (Exod. 19.6); God's care of the Ethiopians, Philistines and Syrians, as well as Israel, was noted by Amos (9.7), and the prophets generally look forward to the day when all nations would worship the Lord (Isa. 2.1–4; 19.19–25; 45.22 f.; 49.6; Mic. 4.1–4). The choice of Israel was a unique act (Amos 3.1 f.) for responsible co-operation with God by faith, as exemplified by Abraham himself, not for privilege alone.

27 : From Clan to People

Genesis 47

Abraham and his family had entered Egypt in a time of famine, apparently stepping out of the circle of God's will.

Now his grandson, Jacob, and his family were back again in Egypt, in yet another such time. The essential difference is that now they were there in accordance with God's predetermined plan, and there were all the signs of His preparation to facilitate their settlement. The remarkable adventures of Joseph, which resulted in his becoming the Prime Minister of Egypt and the saviour of a considerable area during the seven-year famine, had a large part in this. The family of Jacob was not only spared the physical effects of famine, it was given preferential treatment through Joseph's agency, and allowed to settle in the relatively fertile area of Goshen, in the eastern-delta (6). Joseph deliberately sought to preserve the separate identity of his people by stressing that they were shepherds, regarded as inferior by the Egyptians (3 f., cf. **46**.31–34). Moreover, the choice of Goshen would enable them to make an easy get-away when the opportunity or necessity arose. In the years that followed the orientation towards the promised land continued. Jacob himself bore witness to it in the solemn vow he extracted from Joseph concerning his burial in Canaan (29 ff.), and Joseph's last request is to be interpreted in the same light (**50**.24 ff.). The promise to Abraham was obviously taken seriously.

It is instructive to note how God was fashioning a clan into a nation. At first the environment was congenial, and the family of Jacob prospered in a sheltered situation, whilst still preserving their identity (27). Later on the fire of persecution was to weld the Israelites together and then provide the impetus to drive them out from Egypt. This process took time, 400 years in fact, but even this painful period had been foretold in the promise to Abraham (**15**.13 f.). We note again God's sovereign control of history, using economic, geographic and political factors in the outworking of His will.

28 : A Nation is Born

Exodus 14.5–31

More than any other single event in the O.T. the deliverance at the Red Sea became the great, decisive act of salvation to subsequent generations of Israelites, comparable to the centrality of the Calvary-event in the N.T. God was revealed as:

1. The one great, active, personal Power. His control over the forces of nature, and His dominance over the gods of Egypt, symbolized in the various animals, insects and even the sun itself, had been amply demonstrated in the ten plagues. Now again His Lordship is established. It is clear that the gods of Egypt had no effective power, only God has power to act, and that decisively. Israel's role in this crisis was completely passive (14). Again He is seen in control of the forces of nature, the wind and the sea, which operate in precise accord with His will. Miracles are possible to a supernatural God, whether they involve the use, or the temporary setting-aside, of the laws which He has established within nature.

2. The God of Salvation. All His might was employed in the service of His chosen people, an aspect high-lighted by an apparently impossible situation (cf. **14**.3). The crossing probably took place in the vicinity of the modern Lake Timsah, which the Israelites may already have made an abortive attempt to cross (cf. 'turn back', **14**.1 f.). Now completely trapped, their utter helplessness is reflected in their bitter outburst (10 ff.). In a hopeless predicament the God of Salvation dramatically intervened (cf. Rom. **3**.9–23; Eph. **2**.1–6). His protective presence was further revealed in the cloud and the activity of the 'angel of God' (19 f., 24).

3. The God of Grace. His saving acts did not rest on the worthiness of the Hebrews, or even their faith, which appears to have vanished completely in the light of the crisis (10 ff.). The same factor may be noted when Moses was establishing the details of the covenant-relationship directly with God, whilst the people were sinning in the matter of the Golden Calf (ch. **32**). The faith of Moses at the Red Sea was in sharp contrast to his fellow Israelites (13 f.).

4. A God faithful to His promise. This aspect is not expressly stated in this chapter, but it is intimately related to the whole context (**6**.3 f., 8, cf. **3**.8, 17). It was the Lord who, acting in history in a series of unique events, made Israel into a nation. The people had seen the great work of the Lord, and their response was one of belief, fear and worship directed to an incomparable God of Salvation (**14**.31–**15**.2, 11).

29 : Pause for Reflection

Deuteronomy 6.20-25; 7.17-26

Deuteronomy enshrines the magnificent attempt of Moses to relate God's gracious acts in history, and His covenant-relationship with Israel, to the every-day life of the community. It is an appeal to Israel to live as a redeemed people, to accept its high calling and walk worthy of it. It would be advisable to read through the earlier portion of ch. 6, particularly noting vs. 4, 13 ff., which teach the unity and uniqueness of God, and which demand single-hearted loyalty.

Deut. 6.20-25 is probably an early confession of faith (cf. 26.5-9; Josh. 24.2-13). Israel was never to forget its humble origin, which was the background of Yahweh's gracious acts. The deliverance from Egypt, the gift of the land and the fulfilment of the patriarchal promise are all stressed here (21 ff.). The law is not an intrusion into this scheme, but complements it; it is not a burden but a gift of grace, 'for our good always' (20, 24 f.). Acceptance of it and obedience would ensure a continued place in the divine favour, and careful teaching would ensure that future generations would participate in the blessings of the covenant-community (20).

The implications of past history are further worked out in 7.17-26. Faith frequently shrinks at the massive problems and trials which loom ahead, but it is strengthened by remembrance of the great and decisive acts of God. The fact that the Lord God was on their side meant that they were invincible (cf. Psa. 124), and this realization, projected into the future, became the assurance expressed by Paul in Rom. 8.31. The numerical inferiority of Israel is indicated in the gradual way the Lord would enable them to effect the conquest (22-24), which underlines the miracle of the Israelite occupation of the promised land. Once more the events of the Salvation-history were made the basis of an appeal to Israel to give its Saviour uncompromising, whole-hearted allegiance. Idolatry was to be totally eradicated, not even the gold or silver used in the construction of idols was to be coveted; in a literal as well as a spiritual sense Israelites were to 'abstain from every form of evil' (1 Thess. 5.22) and not attempt to serve God *and* mammon. Israel was called to a tremendously high vocation and its subsequent failure is attributable to its disobedience and its failure to allow God the unrivalled place.

FIVE

God and the Nation

30 : The Verge of Fulfilment

Joshua 3.1—4.7

The miracle of the crossing of the Jordan was overshadowed by the more spectacular deliverance at the Red Sea. Yet it was a notable event which occurred at a decisive point in the history of a nation poised to enter the promised land. The significance is emphasized by the minute attention to detail characteristic of the O.T. legislation. God is so high and holy that any haphazard approach to Him is an insult. The people were to keep about a thousand yards distant from the ark, the symbol of the Lord's presence in the covenantal-relationship (3.4). They were also to sanctify themselves (3.5, cf. Exod. 19.14 f.), for the 'living God . . . among you' (3.10) is to be taken seriously. It was this presence which guaranteed continuity and completion; the great Moses had died, but the fulfilment of the promises did not rest on a person, but on the active God Himself, who now marked out Joshua as the human leader (3.7, cf. 1.5, 17).

The crossing of the Jordan took place in Springtime, when, in the Jordan rift-valley, the cereal harvest would be well advanced (15). Comparison with 5.10 shows that it was just before the Passover, when the river would be swollen enormously by the winter rains and the melting snow from the Hermon range. The fords would be impassable and to cross by swimming would be hazardous (cf. 1 Chron. 12.15). Possibly the waters of Jordan were dammed up by the collapse of the steep clay cliffs at Adam (3.16). In 1927 a similar landslide, following an earthquake, held back the waters for twenty-one hours. This in no way denies the fact of divine intervention, which occurred with such precision. Notice how God called for the response of faith to the promised miracle; it was only as the priestly procession entered the waters that a crossing became possible (3.13).

Once over the Jordan, the Israelites would be exposed to the 'seven nations greater and mightier' (Deut. 7.1), and the flood waters they were to cross victoriously could become a death-trap. So the Lord renewed His promise concerning the occupation of the land (3.10), thus giving further assurance to His people. But these manifestations of a 'living God' would strike terror in the hearts of their adversaries (cf. 5.1), for nothing could withstand a God who was so manifestly supreme in nature and history (cf. 2.9 ff.). It is noteworthy that, to the Israelites, the character and nature of God were expressed in His actions. He is still 'the living God', not simply a set of theological propositions or credal statements, and the obligation to pass on to the rising generation what we know of Him by experience is still obligatory (4.6 f., cf. Exod. 12.26 f.; 13.14 f.; Deut. 6.20–25).

31 : The Dark Ages
Judges 2

The high hopes which existed when Israel entered the promised land were soon shattered, and 'the angel of the Lord', which in the O.T. usually denotes the temporary manifestation of the Lord Himself, laid His finger with disconcerting directness upon the reason—Israel's disobedience (1 f.). The covenantal relationship was two-sided, and the continued faithfulness of the Lord contrasts with His people's faithlessness. They compromised their position by failure to remain separated to the Lord, and in spite of clear warnings (e.g. Exod. 23.32; 34.12; Josh. 23.12 f.) they became allied with the Canaanites and inevitably became involved in their religion, a process described in the O.T as spiritual adultery (17, cf. Jer. 2.20–3.14; Hos. 2.1–13). The appropriateness of this terminology is apparent when it is realized that the Canaanite religion was a licentious, polytheistic nature-cult, designed to promote fertility in man, beasts and nature generally. The degree of danger in this apostasy is revealed in the fact that eventually the Jerusalem Temple itself was polluted, becoming the dwelling-place of the cult-prostitutes (2 Kings 23.4–7). So the waywardness and disobedience of the Judges' period was not inconsequential, it was disastrous.

Verses 11–19 summarize the two centuries of the Judges' period, with its wearisome cycle of apostasy, oppression, temporary repentance and deliverance. Four things are especially noteworthy: the sovereignty and righteous judgement of Yahweh who used the surrounding nations to punish His sinful people (14 f.); His incredible longsuffering in responding again and again to their short-lived repentance; His faithfulness in the covenant-relationship, shattered time and again by Israel's infidelity (13, 17, 19 f.); and the utter worthlessness of Israel. The chapter illumines the sheer grace of God manifested in the O.T. period; He was able even to use His people's failure to discipline them (22 f.).

The elevating influence of Joshua and his contemporaries, 'the salt of the earth' (Matt. 5.13), stayed the corrupting influences of Canaanite religion for a whole generation (7, 10). These men *were* obedient, and they remembered the Lord and His mighty acts of grace. The same simple virtues will keep the present generation of the Lord's people from the corrupting influences which abound. Compromise, on the other hand, is always the pathway to disaster.

32 : The Lord is King !

1 Samuel 12

Samuel was an important character in a transitional period. The last of the Judges, he anointed the first two kings of Israel, Saul and David (1 Sam. 10.1; 16.13). He viewed Israel's request for a king as a personal rejection, but a more serious factor was made clear: it was a rejection of the Lord Himself as the true King of Israel (12, cf. 8.7 ff., Judg. 8.23). Samuel's defence of his own conduct and character (1–5) was therefore more than self-justification. It was also a vindication of the Lord's rule through His servant. Samuel continues to plead for the Lord's honour in vs. 6–12, which reviews the events of approximately six centuries! During this entire period Yahweh had exercised His kingly control over and on behalf of Israel, but Israel did not appreciate that His control of history had two facets; it included His use of other nations to chasten His people as well as His saving acts on their behalf. The apostasy characteristic of the Judges' period now manifested itself in a new guise. It questioned the Lord's power in a fresh crisis in which Philistine oppression (chs. 4, 7) was aggravated by the Ammonite attack (11). They thought a monarchy would solve all their problems (8.10 f.).

There was no fundamental opposition to the concept of the monarchy. In fact, the legislation of Deut 17.14–20 provided for this. But the manner in which a king was demanded was altogether alien to the spirit of confident trust in Yahweh alone (19b, 20, cf. 8.7 ff.; 10.17–25). In the longsuffering grace of God this failure became the point of a new challenge and opportunity. The monarchy would not automatically solve their problems. Only loyal, filial obedience would guarantee the divine blessing, but if they and their king would tread this pathway then all would be well (14 f., 20, 24). 'Vain things' (21) is a reference to their idolatry (cf. Isa. 41.29). The faithfulness of the Lord is apparent, particularly in v. 22, where His constancy to His own purpose for Israel contrasts with their fickle attitude. Nor was Samuel cast off, for in the new situation he continued to exercise a mediating, intercessory ministry as the chief representative of Yahweh (19, 23). The sign (16 ff.) confirmed Samuel's place in God's will. No mere man could call up a storm at will in a season when the summer drought was normally well advanced!

A point to ponder. The Lord is always King whatever form of human government may exist. The former is permanent, the latter is transient.

33 : 'He brings down . . . and raises up' (1 Sam. 2.6)
1 Kings 11.26–40

Another dismal chapter of failure is documented in today's section. Samuel had expressly warned the people of the impositions they could expect from a king (1 Sam. 8.10–18). The Book of the Law, which ought to have been treasured by the king, was equally forthright (Deut. 17.14–20). Solomon had broken its precepts. A king of tremendous potential, he began well (e.g. 1 Kings 3.1–10) but ended in degeneration, so that he merits the title, 'the wisest fool in Jewry'. His

ostentatious building projects (**7.1–8**; **9**.15–19) and the extravagance of the court-life in Jerusalem (**4**.22–28) laid a heavy
burden upon his people. Nor was this burden fairly distri-
buted, for Judah was exempted both from supplying court
provisions and from forced labour. The northern tribes bore
the brunt of these impositions, which they bitterly resented.
This led to the shattering of the kingdom after the death of
Solomon (**12**.1–20).

But Solomon's chief sin was in the personal realm, not the
political or the economic. Following the pattern of kingship
in neighbouring countries he built up an immense harem at
Jerusalem (**11**.1–3). Possibly he could plead the example of
his father, David (e.g. 2 Sam. **5**.13; **15**.16), but Solomon's
harem included many foreign women, in complete disobedience of the Lord's command, and in wilful disregard
of the catastrophic effects of this very sin during the Judges
period (Judg. **3**.5 f.). From accommodating his foreign wives
by building altars to their gods (**11**.7 f.) it was but a step to
actually worshipping these false deities (**11**.5, 33). Solomon,
the builder of the Temple and the composer of the beautiful
prayer of dedication (**8**.12–53), the man who had proclaimed
Yahweh as the universal and sole God (**8**.27, 60), now became
an idolator. Such was the end of the perilous path of compromise. The united monarchy crashed because the king,
instead of upholding the honour of the Lord, actually led his
people into apostasy. The disruption of the kingdom was the
divine judgement upon Solomon's folly (31 f.).

In this crisis period God made possible a new beginning.
Jeroboam, the king-designate of the northern tribes (31, 37),
had a golden opportunity to profit from the mistakes of
Solomon, and by his loyal obedience, to be the founder of a
secure dynasty (38). But by his policies (**12**. 26–33) he led
the new kingdom astray and earned for himself the un-
enviable description of the one who made Israel to sin
(**15**.26, 34, etc.).

34 : The End of the Line
2 Chronicles 36.1–21

To describe the monarchy as an unqualified failure is an over-
statement. It is true that in the northern kingdom of Israel

not one king escaped condemnation, and increasing corruption led to its downfall in 721 B.C. (cf. 2 Kings 17). But in the southern kingdom of Judah there were a number of good kings, including the two lesser reformers Asa and Jehoshaphat (1 Kings 15.9–15; 22.42 f.) and the two great reformers Hezekiah and Josiah (2 Kings 18.1–6; 23.1–25). Josiah, in particular, launched a massive reformation, but the prophet Jeremiah, whilst appreciating the king's sincerity (Jer. 22.15 f.; 2 Chron. 35.25), saw that this reformation was merely superficial (Jer. 4.3 f.). Three of Josiah's four sons, Jehoahaz, Jehoiakim and Zedekiah ('brother', v. 10, should be 'uncle', cf. 2 Kings 24.17; 1 Chron. 3.15), reigned during the twenty-two-year period following his death (609–587 B.C.), but not one of them followed his reforming policies. Jeremiah, whose forty-year ministry covered the whole of this period as well as the larger part of Josiah's reign, constantly urged the people to repent, warning them clearly of the consequences of their immorality and apostasy. But they rejected Jeremiah as they had rejected a whole succession of divinely-appointed prophets (15 f.), whilst the priests, ostensibly the representatives of Yahweh, were the ring-leaders in idolatrous practices (14).

By this time Israel had been a nation for nearly 700 years (c. 1270–587 B.C.) but as a covenant-people they had failed dismally to live up to God's requirements, in spite of a succession of godly judges, kings and prophets who had sought strenuously to stay this downward drift. Countless opportunities to reform had been squandered and the warning through the fate which overtook Israel had been ignored by Judah (cf. Jer. 3.6–10). During the last four reigns, covered in our portion, there was a landslide to corruption which engulfed even the Temple itself (14b, cf. 2 Kings 23.4–7). Divine judgement could no longer be deferred and the Babylonians, under Nebuchadnezzar, acted as God's executioners. Preliminary chastisements (6, 10) which ought to have served as warnings were followed by the final desolating overthrow of Jerusalem, its Temple and the Davidic kingdom in 587 B.C. 2 Kings 24.14 f. and Jer. 39.9 f.; 52.28 ff. show that relatively few Jews survived this destruction. It was a severe, but well-merited, judgement, and the Chronicler regarded the seventy-year period of Babylonian supremacy (21, cf. Jer. 25.11; 29.10) as punishment for c. 490 (70 x 7) years of failure. Humanly speaking, all hope had disappeared for Judah.

47

35 : A God Who Works Wonders

Ezra 1

A comparison of 2 Chron. 36.22 f. with Ezra 1.1 ff. shows that the book of Ezra was originally attached to Chronicles; indeed, some leading scholars believe that Ezra was the author of the composite work. Ezra 1 is a thrilling example of the way God works in history to effect His own will. The Jews in captivity were in a seemingly hopeless situation, an insignificant community in the iron grip of Babylon, about 800 miles from their homeland. Ezek. 37.11 illustrates the complete despair of the exiles. But God was still in control of world events and He had certainly not forgotten His people, now reduced to a remnant purified of the blatant apostasy which had caused the national disaster. Through Jeremiah (Jer. 25.11 f.; 29.10) He had foretold the period of Babylonian domination, which may be dated from 605 B.C. (2 Kings 24.1). Now, in 539 B.C., He raised up a new world power, the Medes and the Persians, under Cyrus, which was to overthrow the Babylonians.

Initially, it may have seemed that it was simply a change of masters which would bring the Jews no benefit. But Cyrus, king of the greatest contemporary world-power, was an unusual man with enlightened views, who deliberately reversed the cruel policies of the Babylonians. Archaeology confirms the historicity of Ezra 1, showing that Cyrus allowed other subject-peoples to return to their homelands. More than this, he materially assisted them in re-establishing their native religions. His public relations department was particularly good; the decree of 1.2 ff. was probably drawn up with Jewish help. Isaiah makes it clear that Cyrus himself was not a worshipper of Yahweh (Isa. 45.4). Contemporary inscriptions also reveal that Cyrus allowed the idols of the subject-nations, normally deposited in the conqueror's temple, to be returned to them. As the Jewish faith was imageless, the Temple vessels, which had had an unusual history, were returned instead (cf. 2 Kings 24.13; 25.13 ff.; Jer. 27.16–28.4; Dan. 5.2 ff.). It was a great moment, a stupendous deliverance comparable with the Exodus (cf. Jer. 16.14 f.) when the exiles set out on the long journey to Zion (note how v. 4 links with Exod. 12.35 f.). But it was a new beginning in a more fundamental way; the old nationalistic order had been shattered, to be replaced by a spiritual community moulded by the law. The covenant relationship with Yahweh was now a fact from Israel's side, not a fiction. So, to the wonder of Yahweh's historical acts was added the change of heart in Israel wrought by His chastening rod.

36 : Lessons from History

Acts 7.1–16

The background of Stephen's 'defence' is an illustration in miniature of the tragedy of Israel's history. On the one hand there was the revelation of God's grace and power revealed through His servant Stephen (6.8, 10). On the other there was fierce hostility to any new departure, a stubborn resistance to any fresh appreciation of the implications of Israel's faith. Stephen realized that the new wine of Christianity could not be contained within the old wine-skins of Judaism. It was not an optional refinement to Judaism but a radical departure, a more excellent way, as the epistle to the Hebrews makes clear. Powerful vested interests, however, were concerned with the place and prestige of Jerusalem, and the fears of the Jews on this score are revealed in the accusations of 6.13 f. Like their O.T. predecessors in their spiritual blindness, they attempted to silence the true voice of God, employing the weapons of misrepresentation and innuendo. The trial was as much a travesty as was the trial of Christ.

To call Stephen's speech a 'defence' is a misnomer, for it was not designed to secure his release. Indeed, it implicated him completely in their eyes. In an historical survey it made clear the principles underlying his attitude to the traditional faith, with its ceremonial law and Temple cultus. These principles are :

1. God is not restricted by national frontiers, and certainly He is not confined to Israel. The call came to Abraham in Mesopotamia (2 f.), and He allowed His people to spend centuries in Egypt (6). Nor is He confined to the Temple; throughout this period He was responsive to the individual faith of the patriarchs, etc., which was the essence of true religion. The land and the Temple, by inference, had no permanent place in His purpose.

2. A stiff-necked nation had always opposed the divinely-appointed saviours, as illustrated here by the case of Joseph (9).

3. Frequently in the O.T. period there was the new departure which defies convention and common sense, as in the case of Abraham (2 f.). Obedience to God always overrules the claims of prudence.

4. The forward-look is of greater importance than attachment to the past. It was the promise which sustained Abraham, although he lived and died in a state of unfulfilment, and even the family grave was purchased, not given. The interment of the patriarchal remains in Canaan (16, cf. Gen. 50.13, 25 f.; Josh. 24.32) was an expression of this same faith, as was the conviction that God had power to bring them through seemingly-impossible situations (6 f., 9 f.).

37 : 'Stiff-necked'

Acts 7.17–53

Stephen continues his thesis that Israel had not changed its basically wayward character over the centuries. He shows that God was not confined to a particular place or geographical locality. His promise was not jeopardized because His people were in steadily-increasing bondage in Egypt (17 ff.); Pharaoh might seem to endanger it by his vindictive policies, but God was raising up His own man, in the very household of Pharaoh, to act as deliverer (20 ff.). A further momentous revelation occurred at Sinai (30-34), where the Law was subsequently given (38), and God continued with His people in 'the tent of witness in the wilderness' (44). So much of decisive importance in Israel's history had taken place *outside* the promised land, and independent of a permanent temple. In contrast, Solomon's magnificent temple is passed over very lightly (47-50), with the observation, noted by Solomon himself, that such a structure could not confine a God like Yahweh (cf. 1 Kings 8.27; Isa. 66.1 f.). The inference is that God seeks a worthier habitation than this, one 'not made with hands' (Mark 14.58, cf. John 14.23; 1 Cor. 3.16 f.; 6.19 f.; Eph. 2.21 f.).

Stephen's second main charge was that Israel had so often rejected the divine revelation. Moses himself, the mediator of the Law, to whom the Jews paid such fulsome lip-service, had in fact been rejected twice (27 ff., 39 f.)! In their idolatry (40 f.) they rejected God Himself, an action which led on to the heathen worship which characterized the entire period until the Babylonian exile (43). They had gathered together the writings of the prophets who themselves had all experienced persecution at the hands of their contemporaries (52). Now the Jews, acting in character with their forefathers, had reached the pinnacle of perfidy by judicially murdering the One whom Moses and their prophets had foretold (37, 52). They were hypocrites, guilty by their double-dealing of the very charge they brought against Stephen (53, cf. **6**.13 f.). No wonder Stephen accused them of being no better than the Gentiles (51), for what circumcision implied in dedication and loving obedience was altogether lacking (cf. Jer. **4**.4; **9**.25 f.; Rom. **2**.25–29). In thus ripping away the mask of hypocrisy from his accusers, Stephen showed that he was in the true prophetic succession and he met the same fate as so many of his predecessors (54–60). Israel indeed had *not* changed.

Questions and themes for study and discussion on Studies 30-37

1. In what sense is the promised land one of the 'permanent images' of faith?

2. Consider the dangers of compromise as illustrated in the Scriptures (Judg. **2**; Gen. **14**; **19**; 2 Cor. **6**.14–7.1, etc.).

3. Observe the place of the prophet in Israel, especially in intervening to rebuke kings, etc. (e.g. 2 Sam. **12**; **24**; 1 Kings **11**.29–39; **13**.1–10, etc.). Is there a similar place for the man of God today?

4. What should be the relationship between human government and God's rule?

5. Compare the actions of God in the exodus from Egypt and in the return from exile.

6. Tabulate the lessons which we may learn from a study of Israel's history.

SIX

God and the Individual

38 : A Man in Adversity
Genesis 39

The devout Israelite realized that the same grace, power and
longsuffering which God displayed on the national level were
available to the individual faithful Israelite, however humble
he might be. Since God did not reduce His almighty power
when intervening on the individual level, the distressed
Israelite frequently reminded himself of God's mighty acts of
salvation for Israel (e.g. Psa. 22.4 f.). God is *still* available in
this way and His resources to intervene decisively, in any
situation, are unlimited.

His sovereign control of events is graphically illustrated in
the case of Joseph. Gen. 39 *could* be viewed as the most
discouraging chapter in the O.T. Here a man already in misfortune, rejected by his brothers and sold into slavery in a
strange land, met further cruel blows of fate. Having lifted
himself up by his integrity and industry to a responsible
office in Potiphar's household (1–6) he found himself assailed
by temptation, his successful resistance to which brought him
wrongful accusation and prison (7–20). Surely we could have
excused Joseph had he resigned himself to what seemed the
cruel hand of fate, and ceased to try or trust God! The
secret of Joseph's victory, which first and foremost took place
in his own innermost being, is carefully documented. 'The
Lord was with Joseph' (2, 21). The effect of this divine companionship was so evident that others were impressed (3, 23),
and it was this which kept Joseph silent in the face of false

accusation, steadfast in multiplied misfortunes, and, at all times, serene in his own soul. He was an outstanding example of the truth 'in *everything* God works for good with those who love him' (Rom. 8.28). So this chapter of misfortunes became the decisive experience in Joseph's life. Hitherto he appears as a spoilt, precocious and tactless youth, but from this point there is a maturity and richness of character which, as we have noted, was evident to others. God frequently subjects the man He chooses to do some special work for Him to periods of trial and adversity. This is never arbitrary. It is lovingly designed and controlled to fashion him for his unique ministry. Samuel Rutherford speaks of this preparation, 'Why should I start at the plough of my Lord, that maketh the deep furrows in my soul? I know He is no unwise husbandman, He purposeth a crop.'

39 : The Testing Continues

Genesis 40

Psa. 105.16–19 illuminates this period of testing, during which God took time to fit His servant for his ultimate ministry. This period of humiliation included the vague 'some time' (1) as well as the 'two years' of 41.1. God is never hurried in this regard: forty years elapsed between Moses' first rash attempt to deliver his people and his ultimate return to Egypt as deliverer (Exod. 2.11–15; 7.7); Saul, after his conversion, spent three years in seclusion (Gal. 1.18) and a further period in obscurity until Barnabas sought him out (Gal. 1.21; Acts 11.25 f.).

The evidence of divine companionship continues in ch. 40. In a very lowly and discouraging situation Joseph sought to be the best that he could be (cf. 39.22 f.), and it was this quality which fitted him for the task of universal importance he was ultimately to assume. His faithfulness in very little was the basis upon which God was able to entrust to him matters of great concern (cf. Luke 16.10 ff.). There is a lesson here. So often we lament our obscure circumstances and limited opportunities, envying others their talents, opportunities and position, etc. God expects us to prove ourselves, and, more important, to *prove Him,* in our *present* situation.

It was quite an occasion in the prison-life when two such distinguished prisoners as Pharaoh's butler and baker (officials connected with food and drink were a trusted *élite,* cf. Neh. **1**.11–**2**.1) were admitted. Their station was so far above Joseph's that he was made their personal attendant—a servant of prisoners (4)! Dreams were commonly regarded as omens or prophecies, especially in Egypt, where a whole body of literature on dream-interpretation was available. Hence the gloom of the two important prisoners after their dreams, for they had no access to official sources of interpretation (cf. **41**.8). But Joseph's God was the Lord of all, and no secrets could be hidden from Him (cf. Dan. **2**.22). Notice how Joseph's habit was to refer things to Him *and* to give Him the glory (8, cf. **41**.16). There is something very human in v. 15, 'I was indeed stolen . . .'; he would not want to confess to strangers the humiliating truth that he had been sold into slavery by his own brothers. The forgetfulness and ingratitude of the chief butler (23) were probably hard to bear, but there is no hint that Joseph became embittered by this experience —the Lord is able to keep in every situation.

40 : 'It is not in me; God will give . . .'
Genesis 41.1–45

The authentic Egyptian background of the Joseph narratives confirms their historicity. In ch. 41 this is indicated by: the cows coming out of the river, where they would escape the flies and the heat (2); the word for magician (8), which, as S. R. Driver admits, is 'found only in connexion with Egypt'; the fact that Joseph shaved himself before his audience with Pharaoh (14)—the Egyptians, except those of inferior rank, were normally clean-shaven; and the details of dress and the respect shown to one who was virtually the vizier of Egypt (42 f.).

The outstanding feature of this chapter, however, is Joseph's meteoric rise from obscurity to a place of highest honour. Pharaoh's concern over his two dreams on a similar theme (the repetition would indicate unusual significance) prompted the memory of the chief butler (9–13) and within moments Joseph had left the prison. His relationship to God was not dimmed by the years of affliction. He realized still his utter dependence on God (16) who was sovereignly active in Egypt (25, 28, 32). The loving care of God for all men is noted in the compassionate warning of v. 28. There is no suggestion that the seven-year famine was a divine judgement; it was no more than a natural calamity, but two attitudes were possible in the light of this revelation. One was the fatalistic approach which resigns itself to a situation and does nothing; the other, accepting the situation, takes active steps to minimize its effects (cf. Matt. 24.15–18). Joseph, balancing complete trust in God with a realistic and comprehensive use of his own faculties (themselves illumined and sharpened by his relationship with God), suggested a plan that immediately gained the admiration and approval of Pharaoh and his servants (33–37). Joseph found his situation completely transformed. Only Pharaoh was greater than he in all Egypt (40 f.). The Architect behind this miracle was the Lord Himself, whose hand was upon Joseph in the painful period of preparation as well as in his dramatic elevation. Had Joseph lost faith in the years of adversity, had he exclaimed, 'All these things are against me', and resigned himself to what appeared to be cruel fate, how different the situation would have been! But 'the Lord was with Joseph', and He can be with us too. There is no pathway of adversity so narrow that it separates us from Him; there is no task for which His grace is insufficient; there is no situation which He is unable to use for our own enrichment of character, and thereby He enriches ultimately the whole world.

41 : 'God meant it for good' (Gen. 50.20)
Genesis 41.46—42.5; 45.4–15

A comparison of 37.2 and 41.46 shows that about thirteen years of Joseph's life were spent in slavery or imprisonment. Now, released and promoted to high honour, he vigorously carried out the programme which he had advocated (41.46–49). The names of his two sons show his continuing confidence in the God whose intervention had had so decisive an influence in his life (51 f.). As Ephraim and Manasseh both became the founders of important tribes, Joseph was to have a double portion in later Israel (cf. 48.5–20).

The beginning of the seven-year famine confirmed Joseph's interpretation of Pharaoh's dreams and vindicated the policies he had suggested (41.25–42.5). It was rather unusual for both Egypt and Canaan to be affected by famine simultaneously, since their geographic and climatic features were so different. Just nine years after Joseph's elevation (45.6) ten of Jacob's sons came into Egypt to buy corn—the pointed omission of Benjamin may suggest that Jacob suspected their guilty secret concerning Joseph (42.4). Joseph dealt skilfully with his brothers, satisfying himself of their genuine change of heart and true repentance (42.6–44.17). When Judah offered himself for life-long slavery as a substitute for Benjamin, rather than grieve his father further, there could be no more doubt (44.18–34) and a deeply-moved Joseph revealed himself to his astonished and fearful brothers. He did not gloss over his brothers' sin (45.4 f., cf. 50.15, 20), but he recognized a higher Agency which overruled the human factor. It was *God* who had sent him into Egypt (45.5, 7 f.) and it was *God* who had now made him 'Lord of all Egypt' (45.9, cf. v. 8; note that success had not made Joseph arrogant or proud; he continued to give God all the glory). In a physical sense Joseph was the saviour of many, and God through him preserved His chosen people (45.7) but He also revealed a compassionate concern that reached beyond the family of Jacob (50.20).

The life of Joseph, rejected by his brethren, wrongfully accused and punished, is a remarkable anticipation of the life of Christ. In both cases God used the base motives of men to subserve His purposes (John 11.47–53; Acts 2.23 f., 3.13–17). Christ was crucified by men motivated by their own personal interests and hatred, but in the divine plan this very fact became the means by which salvation was made available to all men. Can you see a further connection between Gen. 41.43 and Phil. 2.9 ff.?

42 : The Divine Vindicator
Psalm 17

We have noted the various misfortunes which assailed Joseph and the fact that he was sustained by his faith in God. The psalm of David which we study today is the type of prayer which Joseph himself could have prayed during his prolonged period of distress, for he, like David, was convinced of his innocence and smarted under false accusation (1–6, 10 ff.). This psalm has been classified as an 'Individual Lament,' a class which, significantly, is the most numerous in the Psalter, for it reflects the natural tendency of finite man to turn, in his need, to God.

David clearly believed in a *personal* God, who was not only available in prayer (6 f.), but who watched over His children with the tender care noted in v. 8. The phrase 'hide me in the shadow of thy wings' has been interpreted in terms of the cherubim in the holy of holies, but a more general reference to the proverbial care of the mother-bird is likely (cf. Isa. 31.5; Luke 13.34 f.). David also believed in a *powerful* God, well able to overcome his formidable adversaries (10–14). But this God was also an *ethical* God, who punishes the ungodly and requires purity of heart and life in those who approach Him in prayer (1–5, cf. Pss. 15.1–5; 24.3 ff.; 51.6–10). The imprecatory element in vs. 13 f. no longer has any place in our prayers (cf. Matt. 5.38–48) but it should be remembered that the psalmist was not seeking a purely private revenge; the honour of God was at stake in such an unwarranted attack on His servant. While he *was* concerned with his own vindication (2), this also involved the open vindication of the God to whom he had entrusted his just cause. So, although his agitation and distress are apparent (cf. the disjointed phrases of vs. 13 f.), the psalmist finally directs his spirit upwards (15, cf. the same progression of thought in Psa. 73). God Himself is the final reward of the one who trusts Him. Some scholars have referred v. 15 to the stage after death, but more likely it points to that present, rich communion with God, unclouded even by the malicious slanders of our enemies, which is the prelude and foretaste of the glory of the after-life.

Questions and themes for study and discussion on Studies 38-42

1. Note some of the other 'decisive experiences' of Scripture (cf. note on Study 38). Has this a parallel in our own lives?
2. Consider the place of discipline and chastisement in the Christian life (cf. Heb. 12.11).

SEVEN

God and the Individual

43 : The Pathway of Rejection

Jeremiah 37

The thrilling life-story of Joseph is true to experience but not representative of all experience. He was a man vindicated during his lifetime by God, and the happy ending of his life more than counter-balanced the bitter years of rejection and slavery. But this is not God's pattern for all His servants. There are many, like Jeremiah, who see little of encouragement or public vindication, men who are required of God to press on faithfully in the face of frustration and opposition.

Jeremiah prophesied in the last forty years of the Davidic kingdom (627–587 B.C.). He consistently proclaimed a message of desolating judgement upon apostate Judah. Without genuine repentance the nation, its capital and the Temple itself would be destroyed. This brought him into unrelenting conflict with a people lulled into false security by their own time-serving prophets, unwilling to accept such an unpalatable ministry as Jeremiah's. The prophet needed peculiar strength to stand firm, for four decades, in such circumstances (cf. 1.18).

This opposition between Jeremiah and his adversaries flared up in the last months of Judah's national life. The eighteen-month siege of Jerusalem, by the Babylonians, had been temporarily lifted by the appearance of an Egyptian army (5, 11), and the king who had refused to accept the prophet's word (2) now sent to him again (3, 7, cf. 21.1 f.), reasoning perhaps that this new event might cause Jeremiah to modify his stern prophecy. On the contrary, Jeremiah announced the withdrawal of Egyptian help and the renewal of the siege and the inevitability of the destruction of Jerusalem (7–10). No doubt the rulers, incensed at Jeremiah's apparently unpatriotic statements, watched him carefully. When he left Jerusalem, possibly to complete the transaction noted in 32.6–15, they falsely accused him of deserting and beat him up shamefully (11–15, cf. v. 20). Zedekiah's action in sending secretly for Jeremiah betrays his personal inclination to obey the word of the Lord (17–21). He had been deceived by his own prophets (19) and led into disastrous, anti-Babylonian policies by his princes. There is a marked contrast between the two men: Zedekiah, the vacillating king, aware of God's word but too timorous to obey it; Jeremiah, the persecuted prophet, still faithful in his unpopular ministry in spite of the shameful treatment he received. In fact, Zedekiah was more bound than his prisoner.

44 : Strength and Weakness
Jeremiah 38
The three principal characters illustrate various aspects of God's dealings :

1. Jeremiah. The prophet's declaration that Jerusalem's fall was inevitable was naturally unpopular with those directing resistance to the Babylonian siege (2 ff.), especially when he counselled desertion to the enemy as the only reasonable course of action if the city itself refused to surrender. But the final accusation of the princes (4b) was a lie; *no one* in Jerusalem had deeper concern for his people than Jeremiah. But he saw clearly the principles underlying God's judgement and knew that there could be no reprieve, although surrender would spare the city and reduce casualties (17 f.). It cost him dearly to stand alone (cf. 15.10), regarded as a traitor, but God gave him the strength to endure. Fearful he undoubtedly was (15, 26, cf. 37.20), and with good reason (4 ff., cf. 11.21; 18.23). Yet he remained true to God and did not hesitate to declare 'the whole counsel of God' (Acts 20.27).

2. Zedekiah, king of Judah in name only, was completely dominated by his princes, whose consistently anti-Babylonian policies ruled out any hope of mercy for them should the city

fall, or surrender (cf. **39**.6). They were prepared to fight to the last even if it involved the utter destruction of Jerusalem. But Zedekiah knew that Jeremiah's oracles were from God; although unpalatable, they were to be obeyed. For a fourth time he sent for Jeremiah (14–23), perhaps hoping against hope that there would be some modification of his stern prophecies. But the word of God never changes unless there be a radical change of heart (**18**.5–10) and this was not forthcoming. Zedekiah destroyed himself and others because he lacked the resolution to obey God. The same cowardly spirit allowed him to hand over a true prophet to his persecutors without protest (5).

3. Ebed-melech was perhaps the most unlikely man in Jerusalem to stand up for Jeremiah. He was just a humble palace slave, an Ethiopian, not a Jew. If the princes and religious officials were united in their opposition to Jeremiah who was he to interfere? Why get involved (cf. Amos **5**.13)? But Ebed-melech *did* get involved, at considerable personal risk, and his protest stimulated the king into taking the only resolute decision recorded of him (10). Ebed-melech's courage was matched by the compassionate way he went about the rescue-operation (11 ff.). His action was noticed by the all-seeing Lord, and at a time when events of international magnitude were taking place, Jeremiah was commissioned to deliver him a personal oracle, assuring him of his safety in the holocaust that was to descend upon Jerusalem (**39**.15–18).

45 : Personal Religion

Matthew 6.1–24

There is always a danger of conventionalizing religion and making it a purely social function, but whilst we cannot eliminate the outward expressions of religion, its true essence must be inward and spiritual, expressive of the individual relationship with God. Their own Scriptures ought to have shown the Pharisees, etc. the futility of lip-service in religion (Isa. **29**.13). But, in fact, they concentrated entirely on the outward forms of almsgiving, prayer and fasting, regarding them as ends in themselves, and not as expressions of a God-ward attitude. Their ostentation in almsgiving (2), prayer (5) and fasting (16), sounds preposterous to us, but we need to search our own hearts. There is always a temptation to display piety and religious acts for the benefit of the onlooker (1 f., 5, 16). The verb 'have' in the clause 'they have their reward' indicates *full* payment; it was used in connection with the receipting of bills. God cannot reward our acts of religion when the motive is simply to gain men's acclaim.

Another danger is the temptation to imagine that God is impressed with quantity rather than quality, whether it be multiplied sacrifices, as in Mic. 6.7, or a spate of words (7). As an example of simplicity and sincerity the Lord gave the great pattern-prayer which commences with concern for God's glory and the extension of His kingdom before passing to man's legitimate needs—physical and spiritual (9–13). Notice again the demand for reality in religion. There can be no forgiveness to the man who, unmindful of the divine forgiveness, refuses to show a forgiving spirit to his brother (14 f.; cf. **18**.21–35; Mark **11**.25).

The vital question is 'Where are our affections?' (19 ff.). Man's heart invariably follows what he conceives to be his treasure. Is our 'treasure' on earth—whether it be the desire for man's applause or material possessions? Or do we see our true treasure in our relationship with God (cf. Psa. **73**.25 f.)? The latter attitude, shown by the man who is 'rich toward God' (Luke **12**.21), illumines the whole life (22 f.). Verses 22 ff. teach the solemn fact that there is no intermediate stage between single-heartedness to God and a consuming love for this world. It is a case of 'either-or'. Lukewarmness is an abomination to Him (Rev. **3**.16). But he who is prepared to give whole-hearted allegiance can safely leave all his material concerns in God's capable hands (see Study No. 34 on **6**.25–34).

46: The Purpose of Suffering

2 Corinthians 1

Paul was no stranger to suffering (cf. 2 Cor. **11**.23–27), but something abnormal had happened to him at Ephesus, and at one point, all hope of survival seemed lost (8 f.). Presumably this had taken place since the writing of 1 Corinthians, so that the experience referred to in 1 Cor. **15**.32 can be ruled out, and in the incident recorded in Acts **19**.23–41 Paul does not appear to have been in great personal danger. There may be a connection with the 'many adversaries' of 1 Cor. **16**.9. But whilst the physical details are obscure the spiritual lessons drawn from this period of acute distress are plain:

1. It brought a new revelation of God as 'the Father of mercies and God of all comfort' (3). The very extremity of his predicament forced Paul to rest the more upon God, and he discovered the immense resources freely available to the Christian. This led to an increased faith in God which replaced self-reliance (9, cf. **3**.5). In the O.T. the supreme illustration of God's power was the deliverance of Israel from Egypt; in the N.T. it is His power to raise the dead, especially Christ (9b, cf. Rom. **1**.4; Eph. **1**.19 ff.).

2. Paul was convinced that suffering endured in the course of Christian service allowed the Christian to enter into the experience of Christ's suffering (5, cf. 2 Cor. **4**.8–12; Phil. **3**.10; Col. **1**.24; Heb. **13**.12 f.). There is, however, a profound difference. The sufferings of Christ were uniquely redemptive. Those of the Christian allow us to demonstrate our gratitude for His supreme atoning work, and grant us greater insight into His passion. Altogether excluded, of course, is that suffering which results from sin.

3. Paul's first-hand experience of God's grace and comfort in his affliction equipped him to minister to others in their distress (4). God often shapes His servants through suffering, nurturing love, sympathy and understanding in the process. We so often put self at the centre, and shrink from suffering, but God sees us in relation to other needy souls. An effective servant of Jesus Christ must be no purveyor of second-hand truths.

4. Paul's concept of the unity of the Church meant that the Corinthians could not only learn and profit from his experi-

ence but that they were actually involved (6 f.). If one member of the body was distressed or comforted, the whole body was necessarily affected (cf. 1 Cor. 12.14–27; Eph. 4.15 f.; Col. 2.19). Since Paul was apparently not completely out of danger, the Corinthians had a solemn responsibility to pray for him (11). Thus suffering has a part to play in accentuating and demonstrating the unity between members of Christ's Church.

47: The Source of Serenity
Philippians 4.10–23

The Philippian church, through one of its members, Epaphroditus, had sent a gift to Paul in prison at Rome (18). Whilst there Epaphroditus himself was critically ill and Paul, to ease the anxiety of the Philippians for their representative, sent him home shortly after his recovery, bearing the Philippian letter (2.25–30). The apostle, anxious to express his deep appreciation of their concern (10, 14 ff.), uses O.T. sacrificial terminology (18, cf. Exod. 29.18; Lev. 1.9, 13, 17), showing that rich, practical fellowship of this kind was an acceptable offering to God Himself.

Yet Paul was in a dilemma. Not wanting to appear ungrateful to his Philippian friends, he was even more concerned to impress the point that he was not dependent upon their gift; he possessed an inward sufficiency which was fundamentally a Christ-sufficiency (11 ff.). 'I have learned' (12) uses a verb meaning 'to initiate', suggesting this was a divinely-revealed secret, not the result of merely human searching or philosophizing. This inward infusion of strength and serenity made him the master of external circumstances. The general background of Paul's life was hardship and persecution (cf. 1 Cor. 4.9–13; 2 Cor. 1.8 f.; 4.7–12; 6.4 f.; 11.23–27; 12.10);· the immediate background was imprisonment at Rome (1.12 ff.), but notice how he includes prosperity (which has caused the downfall of countless Christians) as well as adversity, as conditions over which he has triumphed (12). In an age when a largely-impotent Church is seeking to meet the challenge by improved techniques, streamlined administration and attempts to be 'contemporary', we do well to recall that power for living and service comes only through vital union with Christ (13). The final benediction (23) underlines this same point,

63

that Christ is the sole fountain of grace. Such an endowment is not restricted to the Pauls of the Church, however. The Philippians had access—as have we—to the same inexhaustible treasury (19). The very fullness of God (who can begin to measure it?) is ours (Eph. 3.19)! Such is the extent of God's provision, through Christ, for the individual. When we share the utter confidence and complete committal of Paul in and to such a God we also will be 'more than conquerors' (Rom. 8.37). Verse 20 and its context recall the Westminster Shorter Catechism's definition of man's chief aim—'to glorify God and to enjoy Him for ever.' Ponder carefully the implications of both parts of this quotation.

Another point to consider. The bond-servant of Jesus Christ should live like a king. Do you?

Questions and themes for study and discussion on Studies 43-48

1. Would the purposes of God have been demonstrated more effectively if He had intervened in some miraculous way on behalf of Jeremiah?

2. Consider carefully the relationship between the outward forms and the inward content of true religion (see note on Matt. 6.1–24).

3. Can you think of any other lessons which we can learn through suffering (cf. Study 47 on 2 Cor. 1)? Has the 20th-century Church lost sight of point No. 4?

4. Make a list, in what you feel to be the appropriate order, of the principles which govern God's dealings with the individual.